Richard Emerson is a freelance writer, editor and proofreader, specialising in health-related topics, including diet and nutrition. He is a member of the Medical Journalists' Association, has a Diploma in Biological Sciences and is currently studying for a degree in Natural Sciences with Biology. He has authored four books and contributed to many others.

To Elsie-Louisa for her love,
support and encouragement

READ THE LABEL!
DISCOVER WHAT'S REALLY IN YOUR FOOD

RICHARD EMERSON

Vermilion
LONDON

Published in 2007 by Vermilion, an imprint of Ebury Publishing

A Random House Group Company

Copyright © Richard Emerson 2007

Richard Emerson has asserted his right to be identified as the author of this
Work in accordance with the Copyright, Designs and Patents Act 1988

The Random House Group Limited Reg. No. 954009

Addresses for companies within the Random House Group
can be found at www.randomhouse.co.uk

A CIP catalogue record for this book is
available from the British Library

Penguin Random House is committed to a sustainable future for
our business, our readers and our planet. This book is made from
Forest Stewardship Council® certified paper.

Designed and typeset by seagulls.net

Printed and bound in Great Britain by Clays Ltd, St Ives plc

Copies are available at special rates for bulk orders.
Contact the sales development team on 020 7840 8487
or visit www.booksforpromotions.co.uk for more information.

CONTENTS

ACKNOWLEDGEMENTS

The author would like to thank the following for their invaluable help: David Pickering and Kathryn Heirons of Bucks County Council Trading Standards; David Edwards of Shropshire County Council Trading Standards; Susanna Mordaunt, Sally Pain and Lynda Harrop of the Food Standards Agency; Phaedra Neal of Diabetes UK; Kathryn Miller of Coeliac UK; and Julia Kellaway and everyone else at Vermilion who helped with the production of this book.

FOREWORD

Food is essential to human life, yet the choices offered by the food industry bring many challenges. Consumers are bombarded with information on what to eat and what not to eat from advertisers and food labels. The reality, however, is that most consumers have to make quick decisions when food shopping, and they often switch off and fall back on established habits or half-remembered advice from ill-informed sources.

Transparent and truthful labelling is therefore vital if consumers are to be able to make informed choices, or at least know what they are eating. Without knowledge of how food is produced and labelled, consumers have little or no chance of choosing food that is right for them.

Unfortunately, many parts of the food industry have failed to rise to the challenge of providing clear labelling. They use their resources and energy to promote the most attractive features of the food then hide the negative aspects on the less obvious parts of the package. Sadly, consumers often have neither the time nor the knowledge to unravel the real story behind the label. Trading standards services are responsible for making sure laws controlling food descriptions are followed by retailers and manufacturers. They advise the food industry on how to comply with the legislation and take formal action on the occasions when food providers overstep the mark. However, legal actions are long, complex and expensive, and success is not always guaranteed.

This book is of potential value to the consumer as it distils complicated information into easily digestible chapters. Taking the reader through the common ingredients found in our foods, Richard Emerson also gives his views on how far we can trust the information displayed on labels and provides information to help consumers make informed decisions about the foods they buy.

Highlighting the difference, for example, between 'Use by' and 'Best Before', and what is meant by 'Farmhouse' or 'Home-made', *Read the Label!* provides advice that will give consumers an insight into what really goes into the food they buy and eat.

David Pickering
Joint Lead Food Officer for the Trading Standards Institute; Team Leader, Food and Farming Team, Bucks County Council Trading Standards

INTRODUCTION

WHY READ THE LABEL?

Never before have we had such a wide choice of pre-packed food. Practically every product we buy today comes boxed, tinned or wrapped in plastic and covered with labels. And never before has so much information been printed on the label, which we're expected to digest along with the food. But just how far can you trust it?

Food makers are not allowed to lie but they don't always give the full facts either. There are ways of presenting label data to show a food product in a favourable light while ensuring more unpalatable morsels of information are tucked away where you are less likely to notice them. Food makers needn't have it all their own way, though.

It's time for shoppers to fight back and, armed with this book, you can. In these pages you'll find answers to much-asked questions. *Read the Label!* helps you make informed choices when you shop and it's pocket-sized so you can take it with you.

Labels carry so much information now that, despite all the packaging, food makers have a job fitting it all in. Even some fresh fruit and vegetables come pre-packed with their nutritional content itemised, along with region or country of origin and sometimes even the farmer's name. So, why bother to read the label?

Do we really need to know all this? Well, the plain answer is – yes. Just as we've never had so much information before, we've never before had such a vital need for it. Perhaps the most important reason is that knowing what's on the label can be, quite literally, a matter of life and death.

The number of Britons suffering from food allergies is at an all-time high and, if existing trends are anything to judge by, this is going to increase. Food allergies are often embarrassing, sometimes distressing, always unpleasant and, potentially, fatal. As the list of allergy-triggering (allergenic) foods grows longer, and food processing gets ever more complex, so the risk of encountering a food you'll react to will also increase. To avoid allergens and other problem food ingredients you must read the label.

There's another life-or-death reason why you need to read the label. Diet-related diseases, including obesity and diabetes, are on the increase too. Some cancers are diet-linked, and heart disease is still a major problem. Heart attack rates are actually falling, mainly because fewer people smoke now. But that trend could be reversed as the obesity epidemic spreads and more people suffer from diabetes-linked heart disease.

Labels are packed with information to help you choose healthy foods. They can steer you away from the jagged rocks and swirling whirlpools of excess sugar, salt and fat towards the sun-kissed seas of life-enhancing nutrients. That doesn't mean eating a boring diet, but it does mean being selective. Reading the label helps you choose.

We all want quality products for the right price. Responsible food makers want to give us quality products, for the right profit. In getting the figures to balance, some companies cut corners, bulking up their products with water, gristle, blood, starchy filler, and so on. If you read the label you can spot the dodges.

It would be easy to think that all pre-packed, processed, ready-made food was 'bad for you' and that only food bought from the free-range organic farmers' market down the road was fit to eat. That is misleading. Most pre-packed food is good quality, tasty and poses no threat to the majority of consumers. Even products that are high in salt, sugar and fat are fine for most people – in moderation.

Food makers may think we're too fussy, and that we should be happy so long as we get tasty, nutritious food at a fair price. But consumers *are* getting more fussy, especially over issues such as animal welfare, pesticides, additives, fat, sugar and salt. Consumer groups believe that many food-processing methods used today are the thin end of the wedge and that unless we act now, undesirable practices will become so firmly entrenched they'll be impossible to eradicate.

Food makers don't have *carte blanche* to print what they like. Labelling rules are tougher now so shoppers can be better informed. But there's a long way to go. As shoppers, we must play our part by reading the label and comparing brands – for quality and value, not just price – and use that information to make informed choices.

Labelling information must not give a false impression. If you think you've been misled you've a right to complain to the food maker or local trading standards department. Even if a prosecution seems unlikely, provided enough people complain, the company concerned may well bow to public pressure and revise the product.

Unless, as shoppers, we use our power collectively, we'll lose it to food makers and grocery chains who'll let the profit motive override our interests. Unless we exert our influence on politicians by voicing our concerns and backing those who support our ideals, they'll put the wishes of food makers and grocery chains before ours. The starting point for all this is to read the label and understand what it all means. So, do you want to read the label? Then read on…

1

HOW TO READ
A FOOD LABEL

Not all the information on food labels is compulsory, and so food makers can decide for themselves just how much data they provide. Also, there is little standardisation in food labelling, which is why some food labels are gaudy and wordy while others are dull and uninformative. Some information must be provided by law, however, and the way this is displayed tends to follow a similar pattern.

This chapter will point out the main sections on a 'typical' food label. The product shown here doesn't actually exist (and would be pretty unpleasant if it did) but illustrates some of the features commonly found on food labels, plus a few tricks of the food labelling trade to watch out for. The other chapters deal with these points in more detail and suggest ways to use the information to make informed choices as you shop.

WHAT'S ON THE LABEL?

1. PROMOTIONAL CLAIMS

These are the advertising 'sells' that try to convince you of a food's high quality. They can suggest a long history of successful production ('traditional'), painstaking care ('home-made') or freshness ('natural goodness'). In most cases these terms have no legal meaning so eye them with suspicion (see page 107).

2. BRAND NAME AND/OR DESCRIPTION

This helps you tell one brand from another. In most cases it will identify the nature of the product. *Legally*, though, it doesn't have to. It could be a 'customary' or 'traditional' name, such as 'pizza', or a fancy marketing name, such as 'Acto-Yog'. If the nature of the product is unclear, an accurate name or description (known as its 'legal' name) must, by law, be printed on the label *somewhere* – but it could be in tiny letters and you may have to hunt for it (see page 101).

3. ILLUSTRATIONS

Any photographs or designs on the label must not give a misleading impression. For example, a picture of hens living a carefree life in a sunlit meadow would be misleading on a box of eggs from caged birds. Similarly, any ingredients shown should be in the product – unless, of course, it's just a 'serving suggestion' (see page 107).

4. HEALTH CLAIMS

These are the advertising 'sells' that try to convince you that a product is good for you. They may suggest added goodness ('omega-3', 'high fibre') or a reduction in unhealthy ingredients ('low fat'). Food makers can run into trouble if they tell 'porkies' – but it doesn't mean they won't try to stretch the facts (see page 117).

5. STORAGE AND/OR COOKING INFORMATION

You'll find this information on food products that require special instructions, usually because quality or safety might otherwise be jeopardised. A ready meal may need to be cooked in a microwave rather than an oven, for example, or a food might need storing in a fridge once opened to prevent spoilage (see page 62).

6. ESTIMATED CONTENTS

The label should state how much food there actually is inside all the packaging. If the quantity is followed by an 'e', this means it is an estimate but the figure should be close, otherwise you can complain to your local trading standards department (see page 97).

7. CERTIFIED ENDORSEMENTS

There may be a special logo or certification mark that endorses the food as having been produced according to strict rules laid down by a recognised organisation. The logo might suggest, for example, that a product is suitable for vegetarians ('V') or contains organic ingredients. Food makers must be able to justify claims like this, so if you're unconvinced ask them to prove it (see page 139).

8. ORIGIN MARK

This mark is for safety reasons. If a product is contaminated – with glass or bacteria, for example – the authorities use this mark to trace the food and remove it from sale. The top line is the country of origin

('UK' or 'FR', for example). The middle line is a code identifying the last company in the chain of production. The bottom line indicates that the product meets EC rules. If the origin mark is missing it will have been on an outer wrapper that was removed by the shop before the product went on sale.

9. PRODUCER'S NAME AND ADDRESS

This gives the contact details of the manufacturer, producer or retail outlet. It will provide the registered company name and address and may give a phone number for customers to use. If you have a complaint about a product you should first go to the shop where you bought it. But if you're still unhappy, or have a query the shop can't answer, use these details to contact the company concerned.

10. DATE MARK

The date mark tells you how long a product should last. 'Use by' dates are for foods that go bad quickly – often within days. 'Best before' dates are for products lasting weeks, months or years. Ignore these dates at your peril! (See page 57.)

GRAPE AND CUSTARD FLAVOUR DESSERT

INGREDIENTS; Corn flour, milk (10%), corn syrup, salt, inulin, flavouring (grape, custard), colouring (E110), preservative (E210), stabiliser (E414). **11**

WARNING!

Contains milk. May contain egg, fish, peanut, soya, grape, custa **12**

NUTRITIONAL INFORMATION (AVERAGE VALUES)

	PER 100g	PER 50g SERVING
ENERGY	361 Cals	180 Cals
PROTEIN	12 g	6 g
CARBOHYDRATE	58 g	29 g
(of which sugars)	20 g	10 g
FAT	9 g	4.5 G
(of which saturates)	1.2 g	0.6 g
FIBRE	Trace	Trace
SODIUM	0.2 g	0.1 g
Salt Equivalent	0.5 g	0.25 g

13

GUIDELINE DAILY AMOUNTS

	Women	Men
Calories	2000	2500
Fat (g)	70	95
Saturated fat (g)	20	30

Official Government figures for average adults

14

11. INGREDIENTS

The ingredients list tells you what is actually in the product. It alerts you to healthy and also not-so-healthy contents. If a member of your family must avoid a food ingredient – perhaps because of a dietary disorder such as a food allergy, or a lifestyle decision such as vegetarianism – this is the place to check whether a food is suitable. Food makers may change ingredients from time to time, so regularly recheck the ingredients of brands you buy often, just to be sure (see page 13).

12. WARNING BOX

Some products have a special section that alerts you to any problem ingredients likely to trigger an allergy or food intolerance reaction. This isn't compulsory so don't rely on it (see page 180).

13. NUTRITIONAL INFORMATION

If you're concerned about your family's diet, the nutritional information panel is vital. It lists Calorie content and levels of fat, protein and carbohydrate. Use this information to choose healthier brands or plan a healthy diet for the family. This panel must be shown if a food maker has made a health claim for the product, such as 'low fat' (see page 27).

14. DIETARY GUIDELINE INFORMATION

Many labels now give dietary guidelines to help you plan a healthy diet. Two systems are currently in use: 'Guideline Daily Amounts' (GDAs) and 'traffic lights' (see page 50).

USING LABEL INFORMATION

Later chapters suggest practical ways to apply the label information when buying foods for the family, choosing quality products and selecting 'safe' ingredients for those with particular dietary needs, such as gluten intolerance, food allergies or diabetes.

CHECKOUT...

Just as every shopping trip ends at the checkout, so each chapter in this book ends with a list of points to *check out* as you study the label. Before you buy, read the label and check:

* name or description, so you know what you're buying – it may be hidden
* date mark and storage/cooking details, so you know it's safe to eat
* ingredients and warning box, so you know it's good value and suitable for the family
* nutritional information and dietary guidelines, so you know it's a healthy product that fits in with the family's dietary needs
* promotional claims and endorsements, and decide whether you can trust them.

2

WHAT GOES INTO
YOUR FOOD?

GRAPE AND CUSTARD FLAVOUR DESSERT
INGREDIENTS; Corn flour, milk (10%), corn syrup,
salt, inulin, flavouring (grape, custard), colouring
(E110), preservative (E210), stabiliser (E414).

The 'ingredients' list (or 'contents') is the most
important part of the label. With a few exceptions, it
must list all the food items and chemical additives a
food product contains. In a nutshell, it tells you what
you are actually buying. No matter what the product
is called, or what else may be printed on the packaging, this section must be accurate. It tells you whether
the product contains:

* quality ingredients you want – and in what
  proportion

13

* unhealthy or problem ingredients you're trying to avoid (see page 18).

KEY INGREDIENTS

Ingredients are listed in order of weight or volume – largest first, smallest last. For the most important or 'key' ingredients, the list gives a percentage, such as 'apple (60%)'. Key ingredients are the ones that distinguish one food from another. Without them, a food product would be entirely different. For example, you couldn't have an apple pie without apple. This percentage is the 'quantitative ingredient declaration' (or 'QUID', as it's known in the trade). It shows the key ingredients as a percentage of the whole product. Key ingredients are those that are:

* an essential part of the product, or
* referred to in the name of the product, or
* highlighted on the label in words or pictures.

In a shepherd's pie, for example, minced lamb and mashed potato are key ingredients and so both percentages will be given. You might see them listed as 'lamb (40%), potato (30%)'. (Yoghurt is an exception. Although usually made from milk, you won't see 'milk' listed in the ingredients. But such exceptions are rare.)

This percentage is a useful aid to shoppers. It helps you check whether a product is good value for money (for example, because it contains lots of quality ingredients) or poor value (because it is bulked out with cheap ingredients). It allows you to compare products and discover whether, for instance, one brand of fish fingers is cheaper than another simply because it contains less fish. If you make a note of the percentage of key ingredients in the products you buy regularly, you'll know if food makers are starting to cut corners.

CREAM? THAT'S CRACKERS!

Cream crackers are so called because they once contained 'cream of tartar'. This is no longer the case so, although the word 'cream' is in the title, you won't find any 'cream' in the ingredients. However, as the name is so well-established it is allowed to stay.

If one of the ingredients is a 'compound food' – that is, a mixture of ingredients, such as 'sauce', which could be sold as a food in its own right – the percentage of the key ingredient in the mixture will be listed. So, for example, 'fish in cheese sauce' would show the percentage of fish the product contains *and* the cheese in the cheese sauce. If an ingredient is not essential, and wouldn't be a factor in your deciding whether or not to buy the product, the percentage of that ingredient needn't be given.

Where a product has a traditional or customary name, and not a literal one, the key ingredients are those normally associated with the food. Traditionally, a 'cottage pie' contains beef (not a cottage) and so the label will give the percentage of beef present. If a cottage pie contains lamb it has been mislabelled – that's a shepherd's pie.

Food makers usually work out the percentage based on the weight of all ingredients *before* cooking. However, products such as biscuits, cakes and cooked or cured meats lose water during cooking. In such cases the percentage is based on the weight of the product *as sold*. For example, there might be 50g of butter in 200g of uncooked biscuit mixture. That makes butter 25 per cent of the total mix. But 50g of water might be lost in the baking, so the percentage actually shown on the label would be higher – 33 per cent.

READ THE SMALL PRINT!

Food makers can legally show unappetising infor-mation in tiny type. Why not take a small magnifier with you when you shop?

Meat products sold loose at the baker's, butcher's or supermarket meat and delicatessen counters also need to show the percentage of meat they contain, either on the wrapper or a label nearby, but not their other ingredients. Such products include freshly baked sausage rolls, meat pies and Cornish pasties. This doesn't apply to freshly made meat-filled sandwiches and rolls, meat-based soups, meat salads and all non-meat foods freshly made on the premises. But all products – meat and non-meat – including salads, sandwiches and soups that are prepared elsewhere and sold pre-packed on the premises must display a full list of ingredients on the label.

COMPOSITE INGREDIENTS

So far so good, but the ingredients list can get complicated if a product contains a lot of composite (or mixed) ingredients. This is because each mixture must also list its ingredients, in brackets afterwards, in descending order of weight/volume. For example:

> Fish, sauce (*tomato purée*, *cheese*, *vegetable extracts*, *maize starch*, *Cheddar cheese powder*, *olive oil*), yeast.

Lists with a lot of composite ingredients soon get unwieldy and confusing, especially if one of the ingredients in a mixture is also a mixture. You then have brackets within brackets, making it difficult to work out where one mixture ends and another begins. For example:

> Fish, sauce (tomato purée, vegetable extracts (*tomato, onion, leek, paprika*), maize starch, Cheddar cheese powder, olive oil), yeast.

If you then include the percentages, you end up with...

> Fish (60%), sauce (10%) (tomato purée, vegetable extracts *(tomato (5%), onion, leek, paprika), maize starch, Cheddar cheese powder (4%), olive oil*), yeast.

There's no easy way to untangle this maze. One approach might be to cross through (or underline) all the items between brackets until you are left with the key ingredients. This may help you, in this case, estimate what proportion of the total is made up of sauce.

If the list doesn't give the percentage of an ingredient you are interested in, check where it appears in the list. Remember, ingredients are listed in descending order of quantity so the higher up the list it appears, the more there is.

PROBLEM INGREDIENTS

There are some ingredients you may wish to avoid, perhaps because they're associated with poor quality or unhealthy products. The following are the main ones to watch out for:

BULKING INGREDIENTS

Protein and/or water may be added to bulk out a product artificially. For example, you may see textured vegetable protein (usually soya) on a label. Often called a 'meat extender', this is used to increase the protein content. Sometimes 'foreign' proteins may be added, such as beef protein in a piece of chicken (see page 92).

A little extra water can be added to meat products without being declared on the label (see page 94), but if a product contains more than the legally permitted amount, the extra water must be listed separately. Be suspicious of products that list 'water' in the ingredients. The percentage needn't be given, but its position in the ingredients list is a guide to how much extra water there is. For example, if water is the first ingredient, it means there is more water in the product (by weight) than any other single ingredient.

Additives called polyphosphates (E450) are often added to frozen and chilled chicken to increase the water content. In that case the maximum amount of water allowed is 7.4 per cent. Frozen fish can contain up to 15 per cent water, by weight. If polyphosphates are listed it may be a sign that a meat or fish product has been bulked out with water.

CLARENCE – KING OF CONVENIENCE

Clarence Birdseye, a New York inventor, who died aged 70 in 1956, is best known for frozen fish products. His company, Birds Eye, pioneered the first frozen 'convenience' food – fish fingers. Birdseye invented a way of rapidly *removing* water from food. Today, food technology companies are more interested in ways to *increase* the water content.

FATS TO AVOID

Vegetable fats and oils are added to processed foods to 'improve' flavour, consistency and 'mouth feel'. We tend to think of vegetable oils as being healthier than animal fats. Some, however, including palm oil, are mainly saturated fat, which is linked to disorders such as heart disease when eaten in excess. Even worse are artificial hydrogenated fats.

Hydrogenated Fats and Trans Fats

Hydrogenation is a way of turning cheap vegetable oils into hard fats in order to replace butter and lard in food products. The process involves heating oil to high temperatures and bubbling hydrogen through it. By altering temperature and timings, food makers create mixtures of fats with unique properties – helpful for food manufacturing but not for health (see page 38). Look for 'hydrogenated fats' or 'partially hydrogenated fats' on the label.

Trans fats are a by-product of hydrogenation. They may not be identified by name, but you should assume they're present in any food that contains hydrogenated fats. A European Food Safety Authority report concluded that trans fats are worse than saturated fats at raising levels of harmful LDL cholesterol in the blood and lowering levels of beneficial HDL cholesterol.

Trans fats are linked to obesity, clogged arteries, heart disease, angina and heart attack – a rise of just 2 per cent in trans fats in the diet can increase the risk of heart disease by 23 per cent. Diet experts want UK food makers to list trans fats in products in the UK (as is the case in the USA and other EU countries).

Many UK food makers and grocery chains have pledged to remove hydrogenated fats and trans fats from their products, and some have done so already. Virtually all margarines and spreads are now made using a process that does not produce trans fats.

ADDED SUGARS

Sugar added to pre-packed food is associated with obesity and tooth decay, among other disorders. Added sugar may appear in a bewildering variety of forms, such as brown sugar, corn syrup, demerara, dextrose, fructose, glucose, glucose syrup, hydrolysed starch, invert syrup, lactose, maltose, raw sugar or treacle. The worst of these is corn syrup, often called high fructose corn syrup, or glucose-fructose syrup.

High Fructose Corn Syrup

Fructose is the sugar found in fruit, honey and some cereals and vegetables. In its natural state it is fine for most people, but in a highly processed form – high fructose corn syrup (HFCS) – it is more problematic. Like natural fructose, HFCS is sweeter than sugar but has the same Calorie content (16 per level teaspoon). It is made from corn (maize) in a process that converts corn starch to glucose and then fructose.

Cheap yet versatile, HFCS is popular with food makers. As well as being a sweetener, it makes baked foods go brown (hence its use in cakes, pastries, bread rolls, crackers and breakfast cereals) and it stops ice crystals forming in ice cream.

HFCS is found mainly in highly processed and Calorie-dense products such as biscuits, cakes, cereal bars, cough syrup, fizzy drinks, iced tea, ketchup, meat products, pizzas, sauces, soups and fruit-flavoured yoghurt. A fizzy drink or a carton of yoghurt can contain 12 teaspoons of HFCS (about 200 Calories).

Like all processed sugars, HFCS provides no vitamins and minerals and so is regarded as 'empty Calories'. It may be responsible for health problems in addition to those associated with excess sugar. HFCS fails to dampen the appetite (unlike other sugars) and so its widespread use may be aiding the obesity epidemic. (Obesity rates have doubled in the 25 years since HFCS was introduced.)

It may even be a factor in 'central obesity' – the tendency to accumulate fat around the belly (apple shape) rather than the thighs and bottom (pear shape), a problem now common in women as well as men. Central obesity is linked to an increased risk of heart disease and type 2 diabetes.

ARTIFICIAL SWEETENERS

Artificial sweeteners are increasingly being used instead of added sugar, but some can be problematic. Artificial sweeteners include acesulfame-K, aspartame, saccharine, sodium cyclamate, sorbitol and thaumatin.

Aspartame is added to low-Calorie products, such

as chewing gum, yoghurt and 'diet' soft drinks. Some studies using animals have suggested a potential cancer risk from using aspartame but other studies have concluded it is safe. Current UK government and EC advice is that it poses no significant risk.

However, it does pose a serious risk to a small section of society. Aspartame contains the amino acid phenylalanine, which is toxic to the one in 16,000 children who suffers from the inherited disorder phenylketonuria. Most children make an enzyme that converts phenylalanine into tyrosine, another amino acid. But sufferers produce a defective form of the enzyme, so phenylalanine can build up to toxic levels that cause brain damage. Newborn babies are checked for phenylketonuria. A small blood sample is removed, usually from the heel (called the 'Guthrie test'), which is analysed in a laboratory.

Bulk sweeteners include isomalt, lactitol, maltitol, mannitol, sorbitol and xylitol. They are found in foods marketed as 'diabetic foods', 'tooth-friendly sweets' and 'sugar-free sweets'. They carry the warning 'excessive consumption may produce laxative effects'.

Cyclamate is a sweetener used in soft drinks. Parents are advised to restrict young children's intake of cyclamate because of safety fears (see 'acceptable daily intake', page 162). Children from 18 months to four and a half years should have no more than 180ml (three beakers) of very dilute soft drink or squash per day, or avoid cyclamate drinks altogether. Look for cyclamate, cyclamic acid and E952.

ADDED SALT

Salt is known chemically as sodium chloride and so may be listed as either 'salt' or 'sodium' or both. It is the sodium in salt that, in excess, is bad for you. High salt/sodium intake can lead to high blood pressure, heart disease and stroke. Salt is added to many foods – both sweet *and* savoury. Always check the salt content of food you buy and keep within healthy limits. This is especially important for young children as the amount they can safely consume each day is much lower than the threshold for adults, and yet foods targeted at children are often very salty (see page 152).

OTHER PROBLEM INGREDIENTS

You may need to avoid some ingredients, perhaps because they cause food allergy or food intolerance symptoms in a family member (see page 179). The label must also list chemical additives. Some additives cause side-effects such as hyperactivity in children (see pages 161–178).

CHECKOUT...

The ingredients list is now much more detailed than it used to be and so is well worth studying. By law, the list must be complete and accurate. As you read it, check:

* key ingredients – shown as a percentage
* whether the product contains key ingredients you expect to find – or just flavouring
* key ingredients against other brands – both cheaper and pricier ones
* where other ingredients appear on the list – the *higher* they are, the *more* there is
* if there are 'bulking' ingredients such as added water, proteins and vegetable starch
* if there are ingredients to avoid such as hydrogenated fats, trans fats, corn syrup, excess salt and some sweeteners.

See also allergens (page 182), food intolerances (page 197) and additives (page 161).

3

HEALTHY AND
NUTRITIOUS

NUTRITIONAL INFORMATION (AVERAGE VALUES)		
	PER 100g	PER 50g SERVING
ENERGY	361 Cals	180 Cals
PROTEIN	12 g	6 g
CARBOHYDRATE	58 g	29 g
(of which sugars)	20 g	10 g
FAT	9 g	4.5 g
(of which saturates)	1.2 g	0.6 g
FIBRE	Trace	Trace
SODIUM	0.2 g	0.1 g
Salt Equivalent	0.5 g	0.25 g

The nutritional information box gives the average
quantities ('typical values') of the major nutrients, or
'macronutrients' (carbohydrates, fats, proteins and so
on), in a product. It doesn't tell you what kind of
nutrients the food contains (read the ingredients list
for that); it just gives total amounts so you know how
much fat, for example, is present. Information is
presented in a standardised way so you can easily
compare one product with another.

Food makers don't have to provide a nutritional information box unless they are making a health claim such as 'low Calorie', 'low fat', 'high fibre', 'low salt', 'high in vitamins' and so on. If they do make such a claim they must list the average quantities of all the major food groups – protein, carbohydrate and fat – not just those that justify the claim. This is important, otherwise food makers could claim a product was, for example, 'low in salt' and not show that it was also high in fat.

NUTRITIONAL INFORMATION

Nutritional information is often shown in two columns: one is 'per 100g' and the other 'per serving' (or 'portion', 'item' and so on). The two sets of figures have different jobs:

'PER 100G/LITRE'

This column shows how much of a nutrient would be found in 100g (of solid food) or 100ml (of liquid food) of a product. It lets you compare different brands or products. For example, to see which of two brands of a ready meal had the fewest Calories, you would look at the figures in the 'per 100g' column.

You could also use this column to compare the fat content of two very different products, such as a cream cake and a packet of biscuits. If the cake contains 10g fat per 100g, and the biscuits contain 5g fat per 100g, the cake is twice as 'fatty' as the biscuits.

This is an easy way to make general comparisons. Bear in mind, though, that you might not eat the same amount of, say, biscuits as you would cake – or you might eat more. This is where 'per serving' comes in.

'PER SERVING'

This column helps you decide how much of an ingredient – fat, say – you would actually consume if you ate that product. It normally specifies the serving size ('per 60g serving') or item ('per biscuit', 'per roll', 'per half pack'). You might decide, for example, to buy some Belgian chocolates because, although they are high in fat, you would have only a few, thereby consuming a relatively small amount of fat. But you might reject a cream cake because, although it contains less fat per 100g than the chocolate, you would eat more of it and so consume more fat overall. 'Per serving' can also help with daily diet planning if you make a note of how much fat, sugar and so on you eat each day.

WHAT'S YOUR SERVING SIZE?

Make sure the figure given for a 'serving' is the amount you would actually eat. For example, the nutritional information box may say that a food contains 3g of fat 'per 30g serving'. But if you actually eat 60g of the product you are consuming 6g of fat, not 3g. If in doubt, weigh the amount you normally eat.

ENERGY

This section refers to 'food energy'. The link between food energy, physical activity and weight gain (or loss) is straightforward. You must burn energy daily to stay alive and be active. If you consume more energy than you use you put on weight. If you consume less you lose weight. That's the easy part. The tricky part is knowing how much energy you need.

The 'energy' section gives the figures as kJ (kilojoules) and/or kcals (kilocalories). Ignore kJ/kilojoules – only scientists use them. The figure we're interested in is 'kcals' or 'kilocalories' – regard them both as Calories (see box).

CALORIES

Strictly speaking, what we all call a 'Calorie' is actually a kilocalorie (that is, 1,000 calories). A 'calorie' (usually with a small 'c') is a tiny unit of energy and rarely used. Dietitians and nutritionists talk about 'Calories' (usually with a capital 'C'), not kilocalories.

To monitor your daily energy intake you'll need to add up the Calorie content of all the foods and drinks you consume each day, which can quickly become a chore. The energy section is probably best used to make comparisons between products so you can choose a product that is, say, lower in Calories, and keep high-Calorie products as a rare treat.

MACRONUTRIENTS

The next section of the panel deals with major food components – or 'macro' nutrients. The main macronutrients are protein, carbohydrates and fat. Within the carbohydrate and fat sections there may be further subsections. 'Micro' nutrients – that is, vitamins and minerals, which are eaten in 'micro' amounts – may be listed too (see page 47).

Protein

The 'protein' section is the simplest to follow as there are no subsections. The figure, shown in grams (g), gives the total amount of protein in the product, whether from animal or vegetable sources. Protein is found in most foods, not just meat, fish and eggs.

Cheese is up to 26 per cent protein (higher than chicken – average 25 per cent). Some plant foods are rich sources of protein. Low-fat soya flour is up to 45 per cent protein. Other sources of plant protein include pulses (peas, beans and lentils), nuts, wheat and rice. A slice of wholemeal bread contains around 3g of protein.

You need to eat some protein each day to replace what is lost. Rapidly growing teenagers, physically active people and those recovering from injury or illness have extra demands for protein. If you eat too little protein for your needs, the body takes it from elsewhere, for example by breaking down muscle, to make up the shortfall.

In the UK today, however, most people who eat a

balanced diet get all the protein they need. In fact, the typical UK diet contains too much protein, which can cause problems. First, animal proteins, such as lamb and pork, are high in saturated fat, which should be eaten in moderate amounts only. Excess animal protein is associated with osteoporosis, bowel cancer and other disorders. Second, the body can't store excess protein, so what it doesn't need to replace worn-out proteins is broken down for energy or stored as fat. This means extra work for the liver, and creates excess nitrogen that must be diluted with water and disposed of in the urine, making more work for the kidneys.

Health experts say that no more than around 12 per cent of the average person's daily food intake should be from protein – meat, fish and 'alternatives' (such as peas, beans and lentils). The following chart shows recommended average daily protein intakes for children and adults, by age and sex:

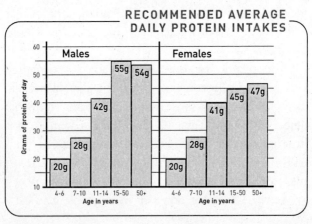

RECOMMENDED AVERAGE
DAILY PROTEIN INTAKES

Good animal protein sources include chicken, turkey, fish, meat, offal (liver and kidney), cheese and milk. It is a good idea to include plant sources of protein too, such as beans, peas and lentils, as these provide other important nutrients like vitamins, minerals and fibre. A serving of cooked lentils contains around 9g of protein.

VEGETARIAN PROTEIN

Vegetarians get some protein from eggs and dairy products. Vegans eat no animal protein and may have more difficulty getting all the essential amino acids they need as some plant proteins don't provide the full range. A good mix of the following sources of protein, if tolerated (see page 179), should be included in vegan/vegetarian diets:

* wheat, rye and oats (for example, from bread, pasta and porridge)
* mycoprotein (such as Quorn™)
* nuts and seeds
* peas, beans, lentils and other pulses (including soya, tofu, miso and soya milk).

Other good sources of plant protein include buckwheat, quinoa and wild rice.

Carbohydrate

This section of the nutritional information shows total carbohydrate in the product. There may be only one figure or it may be broken down into starchy foods (complex carbohydrates) and sugars (simple carbohydrates). Starchy carbohydrates are important energy foods. Wholemeal types are best as they have the all-important vitamins, minerals and fibre needed for good health.

'Of which starch'

This section includes all the starch derived from bread, potatoes, rice and pasta, as well as less common types, such as corn (maize), sweet potatoes, plantain and so on. It may include 'pure' starch such as cornflour, added during manufacture. Starchy foods should make up a third of the diet, at least half of which should be whole grain types.

Starchy foods provide energy at a slow, steady rate to keep you mentally alert and physically active. Whole grain types keep you feeling full for longer, so you are less likely to snack on high-fat/high-sugar foods. This helps you avoid excess weight.

'Of which sugars'

This section includes all sugars present, both 'natural' (that is, found naturally in fruit, vegetables and milk) and those added during manufacture. Natural sugars are known as 'intrinsic' and may be listed as such on the label. Milk sugar (lactose) is not an intrinsic sugar as such but acts like one and so is usually included in this category.

'Added sugars' are sugars extracted from plant cells by processing and so are called 'extrinsic'. You may see them listed as 'non-milk extrinsic sugars' (NMES) on the label. Look at the ingredients list to establish which 'added sugars' are included. Common types include corn syrup, dextrose, fructose, glucose, glucose syrup, honey, invert syrup, lactose, maltose, molasses and sucrose.

Foods high in added sugars contribute to weight gain and are a major cause of gum disease and tooth decay. Although they give a quick energy boost, this may be followed by a slump, leading to fatigue, lethargy, difficulty concentrating and headache (which is why starchy foods are better for you).

'Added sugar' may not be shown separately from 'natural sugar' so it can be hard to check how much 'added' sugar there is. In such cases refer to the list of ingredients. If a product is high in sugar but not high in fruit, you can assume most of the sugar is 'added'.

HOW MUCH ADDED SUGAR?

The recommended maximum intake of 'added sugar' is 10–11 per cent of total Calorie intake:

Women   50g (about 12 teaspoons in total)
Men   65g (about 16 teaspoons in total)

Figures based on FSA guidelines.

If you are trying to cut down on added sugar you'll need to take into account all the sugar in non-diet soft drinks, added in home cooking, sprinkled over breakfast cereals or spooned into hot drinks. If you like a teaspoon of sugar with your tea and you drink six cups a day, that's 24g of sugar consumed daily. If you also enjoy biscuits, cakes and desserts, you'll soon increase that figure (and your own).

Sugar is often added to savoury foods too, such as burger buns, baked beans, sauces, ketchup and ready meals. One way to reduce your intake of added sugars is to use sweeteners (see pages 22 and 173). Natural sugar from fruit and juice is not included in the recommended limit for added sugar, but if your diet contains a lot of fruit and fruit drinks it is advisable to reduce your consumption of added sugars to compensate.

TOO MUCH SUGAR?

Use the following guide to see if there's too much total sugar in a food product:

Per 100g

High 😞	Medium 😐	Low 😊
15g or more	4–14g	5g or less

Figures based on FSA guidelines.

Fat

This section of the nutritional information shows the total amount of fat or oil. Some fats are harmful in excess while others are beneficial in moderation. 'Essential fatty acids' are, as the name suggests, essential for health so it is important that the diet contains enough of them. Many fats also contain vitamins and minerals. So we must all consume some fat, but the UK diet in general is much too 'fatty', which contributes to excess weight and other problems.

The recommended total daily intake of fats is 95g for men and 70g for women. The average UK consumer gets 35 per cent of their food energy from fat. It is so easy to consume excess fat without realising. The British Heart Foundation has calculated that the average packet of crisps contains 3½ teaspoons of cooking oil, and that a daily packet of crisps adds up to 5 litres of oil a year.

TOO MUCH FAT?

Use the following guide to see if there's too much fat in a product:

Per 100g

High ☹	Medium 😐	Low ☺
20g or more	around 4–19g	3g or less

Figures based on FSA guidelines.

The fat section may be the most complex on the label as it is often divided into subsections and even sub-subsections. Fat can be listed as saturated or unsaturated, and there are different kinds of saturated and unsaturated fats. Therefore, total fat may be broken down into:

'Of which saturates'

'Saturates', or saturated fats, are also known as 'hard fats' because they are solid at room temperature. Traditionally, saturated fat in the diet came mainly from 'farmyard' foods like beef, lamb, pork, chicken, turkey, milk, cream and cheese. Increasingly, though, food makers use vegetable forms, such as palm oil and coconut oil, in biscuits, cakes, desserts and ready meals.

Saturated fat should make up only a small proportion of the total daily intake of fat as it raises blood cholesterol levels and so is linked to heart disease and other health problems. Currently, the average Briton gets 13 per cent of total food energy from saturated fat. Ideally, this should be cut to below 11 per cent.

The figure in the 'saturated' fats section will normally include any cholesterol and trans fats present, but these may be listed separately:

'Of which cholesterol'

Cholesterol in the diet is not thought to be as harmful as trans fats and other types of saturated fats. This may seem surprising, as high blood cholesterol *is* harmful. Cholesterol found in the blood is mostly made in the liver from other types of saturated fat. Not much comes from the diet. If you eat foods containing 'natural' cholesterol, the liver tends to produce less cholesterol to compensate.

'Of which trans fats'

Trans fats are found in some meat and dairy products

but are not thought to be so harmful from these sources, provided you don't eat too much. Trans fats are mainly produced by hydrogenation (see page 20). These trans fats are even more harmful than saturated fats and so should be avoided.

TOO MUCH SATURATED FAT?

Use the following guide to see if there's too much saturated fat in a product:

Per 100g

High 😞   Medium 😐   Low 😊
5g or more   around 2–4g   1g or less

Figures based on FSA guidelines.

'Of which unsaturates'
This subsection (if present) gives the total unsaturated fats (or oils) present. Unsaturated fats are found naturally in plant products such as seeds, nuts and some berries and are more beneficial to health than saturated fats. They should make up the majority of the daily fat intake. Don't have too much unsaturated fats and oils, though, as this can still lead to excess weight. The two main types of unsaturated fat are monounsaturated and polyunsaturated. They may be listed separately, as follows:

'Of which monounsaturated'
Monounsaturated fats (oils) used in processed food are mostly rapeseed or olive oil. If the label says 'pure

vegetable oil' it's probably rapeseed oil, but check the ingredients list to be sure. Olive oil is not pure monounsaturated oil. Typically, 'extra virgin' olive oil contains around 75 per cent monounsaturated, 15 per cent saturated and 10 per cent polyunsaturated oil (but proportions vary). Monounsaturated fat has a neutral effect on blood cholesterol, neither raising nor lowering it.

OILING THE FOOD INDUSTRY

Rapeseed oil was once used for oiling steam engines but is being used increasingly in food products. It is made from the seeds of a variety of rape plant (a member of the cabbage family) that was selectively bred to be low in unpleasant tasting or potentially harmful ingredients, such as erucic acid. In North America, rapeseed oil is called 'canola', which stands for Canadian oil low acid.

'Of which polyunsaturated'

Polyunsaturated fat/oil mainly comes from sunflower seeds, peanuts, almonds, walnuts, soya beans and the spreads and cooking oils made from them. It is also found in oily fish, safflowers, linseeds (flax seeds), sesame seeds and maize. Check the ingredients to find out which source is in a product.

Polyunsaturated fats and oils tend to reduce blood cholesterol levels and so help protect against heart disease. Bear in mind, though, that polyunsaturated fats are *less* efficient at *lowering* blood cholesterol levels than saturated fats are at *raising* it – so eating extra polyunsaturated fats won't compensate for a diet high in saturated fat.

For maximum heart protection, around half the fats (oils) in the diet should be polyunsaturated. Certain types – omega-6 and omega-3 oils – are essential fatty acids and so must be obtained from the diet. They may be listed separately as follows:

'Of which omega-6 oils'

Nuts and seeds, and the cooking oils derived from them, are rich in omega-6 oils (also called linoleic fatty acids). At least 1 per cent of an adult's average daily food energy should come from omega-6 oils. However, most of us get far more than that from the cooking oils used in processed foods. In contrast, the average UK diet is deficient in omega-3 oils (see below). The ideal ratio of omega-6 to omega-3 in the diet is four to one or less (that is, no more than 4g of omega-6 for every 1g of omega–3 we eat). In the UK this ratio can be more than ten to one. This imbalance is linked to chronic disorders such as asthma and arthritis and even life-threatening conditions such as cancer and heart disease.

'Of which omega-3 oils'

Omega-3 oils ('fish oils') are found in oily fish and other sea foods. Some omega-3s are found in green leafy vegetables, linseed oil, rapeseed oil, soya and walnuts, but these are a different type (alpha-linolenic acid or ALA) and may not be so beneficial.

The body converts omega-3 oils into the essential fatty acids EPA and DHA (see below). These are vital for the development of a baby's brain and may aid brain function in older children and adults too. They also help protect against heart disease and relieve painful joint conditions. Many food makers are keen to highlight these benefits, and so omega-3s are often listed separately in the nutritional information box.

Although oily fish are a good source of omega-3s, some types contain small amounts of mercury and other toxins. Children and adults, especially women of childbearing age, should limit the amount of oily fish they eat to reduce the slight risk this poses (see box, opposite).

Ideally, at least 0.2 per cent of an adult's average daily energy intake (around 450mg or nearly half a gram) should come from omega-3 oils. This is equivalent to two portions of fish (one an oily fish) per week. Many food makers add omega-3s to products such as yoghurt and bread (see page 125) but these may contain only small amounts and so it is easier to get your recommended intake from natural sources.

DHAs and EPAs

To complicate matters further, the 'omega-3' section may be broken down to give the amounts of two special types of oils called DHA and EPA. These are thought to be particularly beneficial for the brain,

OILY FISH – HOW SAFE IS IT?

Most food experts agree that oily fish is too beneficial to be avoided because of a slight risk from a build-up of toxins. However, health experts recommend limits, especially for children, and women who might become pregnant (whether or not they are actually trying for a baby). Oily fish most often eaten in the UK are anchovies, bloater, eels, herrings, kippers, mackerel, pilchards, salmon, sardines, sprats, trout, tuna (steaks) and whitebait. Girls and women of childbearing age (especially if pregnant or breastfeeding) should have a maximum of two portions of oily fish a week.

Males and older women should limit their intake to four portions a week. Fish at the top of the food chain, such as marlin, shark and swordfish, can contain higher levels of toxins and so should be avoided by children and women of childbearing age. Men and older women should limit how much they eat to no more than one portion a week.

In the case of tinned tuna, processing and canning removes much of the oil and most of the toxins and so it doesn't carry the same risk as fresh tuna. However, women of childbearing age and especially pregnant/breastfeeding women should have no more than four tins per week. There is no limit set for men and older women. There are no general risks associated with white fish and so no limit has been recommended.

especially in children. These long-chain fatty acids have long names to match (DHA stands for docosahexaenoic acid and EPA stands for eicosapentaenoic acid). DHAs and EPAs have unique properties: they are incorporated into cell membranes in the brain, spinal cord, nerves, retinas and optic nerves and may improve concentration, learning and behaviour in children. EPA also protects the heart.

Fibre

Fibre comes from plant-based foods and will be listed in the nutritional information box if the product claims to be high in fibre. Ideally, most adults should consume at least 18g of fibre daily, which is around double the amount in the average UK diet, and some experts recommend as much as 24g or more per day.

Dietary fibre is in two forms: soluble and insoluble. Soluble fibre is found in pulses (peas, beans and lentils), oats, fruit and vegetables. Insoluble fibre (or 'roughage') is mainly found in whole grain cereals and breads, peas and beans.

FLUID AND FIBRE

If you eat a lot of insoluble fibre, drink plenty of fluids to avoid the risk of severe constipation and intestinal blockage. If you're trying to put back weight you've lost, after illness for example, or you have a small appetite, avoid having too much fibre in your diet as this can bulk out your meals and stop you getting all the nourishment you need for good health.

Soluble fibre (especially from oats) attaches to cholesterol released into the gut and stops it being reabsorbed. This lowers blood cholesterol levels and reduces the risk of heart disease. Soluble fibre also helps regulate blood glucose levels. Insoluble fibre absorbs lots of water and so helps bulk out waste matter in the bowel. This prevents constipation and may cut the risk of bowel cancer. High-fibre foods help fill you up without contributing Calories, making it easier to maintain a healthy weight.

Fibre may be listed as 'non-starch polysaccharide' (NSP). Starchy carbohydrates and fibre are both called 'polysaccharides' (which simply means lots of sugar molecules joined together in a chain), so fibre is called 'NSP' to tell it apart.

ENOUGH FIBRE?

Use the following guide to see if there's enough fibre in a product:

Per 100g

High ☺	Medium ☺	Low ☹
3g or more	around 1–2g	0.5g or less

Figures based on FSA guidelines.

Salt (Sodium)

Salt is also known as sodium chloride, so the label may say how much salt or sodium or 'salt equivalent' is present. To convert sodium to its 'salt equivalent' multiply by 2.5. It is the sodium in salt that is potentially bad for you. Too much leads to high blood pressure, heart disease and stroke. The average adult consumes around 9–10g of salt per day. However, the recommended intake is lower:

	Salt/day	Sodium/day
Women	5g	2g
Men	7g	2.8g

Most of the salt (75 per cent) we consume each day comes from pre-packed foods. Ready meals, snacks, sandwiches and fast food are often high in salt. Salt is also found in some sweet foods, such as cakes and biscuits. The rest of the salt we eat is added to home-cooked meals and at the dinner table. So, if you buy food products low in salt avoid compensating by sprinkling extra salt over your meal.

If you like salty food, the best way to cut your intake is to reduce the amount you add to meals gradually, to give your palate time to adjust. Add non-salty sauces, herbs and spices for extra flavour. 'Low sodium' salt is available, but don't be tempted to switch to other sodium-based alternatives, such as monosodium glutamate (MSG), as they can be just as harmful. To compare the saltiness of two foods, look at the level of sodium/salt per 100g. To work out how much salt you would actually consume if you ate the product, look at the amount of salt/sodium per serving.

─────── **TOO MUCH SALT?** ───

Use the following guide to see if there's too much salt in a product (sodium in brackets):

Per 100g

High ☹	Medium 😐	Low ☺
1.5g or more	around 0.4–0.2g	0.3g or less
(0.6g or more)	(around 0.3g)	(0.1g or less)

Figures based on FSA guidelines.

MICRONUTRIENTS

The nutritional information box may also list important micronutrients (vitamins and minerals), especially if health claims are being made for the product. Breakfast foods, for example, are often fortified with micronutrients and so the vitamins and minerals section may be more comprehensive than on the label of other products. These figures are based on a system called 'recommended daily amounts' (RDAs). This sets various benchmark figures for levels of micronutrients that the 'average' person should get from the daily diet. These needs change according to age or circumstances, such as pregnancy.

Most minerals and vitamins are measured in milligrams. But some are needed in very tiny amounts in the body and so may be measured in micrograms.

＊ 1 gram = one thousand milligrams (abbreviated to mg)

∗ 1 gram = one million micrograms (abbreviated to mcg or μg).

───── RDA AND RNI ─

'Recommended daily amount' (RDA) is a relatively old system but is still widely used for food labelling. To confuse matters, a newer system called 'reference nutrient intake' (RNI) is often used by food experts, and some products feature another system altogether: 'international units' (IUs).

As usual, vitamin and mineral levels are shown in two columns – 'per 100g' and 'per serving'. Alongside these are percentage figures (%) indicating the proportion of the RDA each one represents. For example, it might say (per serving):

B1 (thiamin) – 1.2mg – 85% RDA

That means a daily serving of that product will give you almost all the B1 you need. The shortfall should be easy to make up from other foods.

Vitamin and Mineral Chart

Use the chart opposite to check if a food is a 'rich source' of vitamins and minerals – containing at least 50 per cent of the average adult's recommended daily amount (RDA) – or contains the maximum RDA – 100 per cent. The figures are in milligrams (mg), with micrograms (mcg) shown (in brackets) where applicable.

Vitamins	50% RDA mg (mcg)	100% RDA mg (mcg)
A (retinol)	0.4	0.8
B1 (thiamin)	0.7	1.4
B2 (riboflavin)	0.8	1.6
B3 (niacin)	9	18
B5 (pantothenic acid)	3	6
B6 (pyridoxine)	1	2
B9 (folic acid)	0.1	0.2
B12 (cobalamin)	0.0005 (0.5)	0.001 (1)
C (ascorbic acid)	30	60
D (calciferol)	0.00025 (2.5)	0.005 (5)
E (tocopherol)	5	10
H (biotin)	0.075 (75)	0.15 (150)
K (phylloquinone)	0.4 (400)	0.8 (800)

Minerals	50% RDA (mg)	100% RDA (mg)
Calcium	400	800
Copper	0.75	1.5
Iron	7	14
Magnesium	150	300
Manganese	2.5	5
Zinc	7.5	15

DIETARY GUIDELINES

GUIDELINE DAILY AMOUNTS

	Women	Men
Calories	2000	2500
Fat (g)	70	95
Saturated fat (g)	20	30

Official Government figures for average adults

Dietary guidelines shown on food labels – known as 'guideline daily amounts' (GDAs) – can help shoppers relate the products they buy to what is regarded as a healthy daily diet for the average person. GDAs were introduced by the Institute of Grocery Distribution (an advisory body set up by the food and grocery industry itself), based on nutritional research. GDAs often appear on the backs of packs, next to (or a part of) the nutritional information box. GDAs are voluntary, however, so may not be shown at all.

The GDA box might say, for example, that a single serving of a product contains 30 per cent of an adult's 'guideline daily amount' of fat. Shoppers can then use the information to decide whether or not to buy that product.

The system originally covered just Calories, fat and saturated fat for men and women. Now it has been expanded to include carbohydrates, total sugars, protein, fibre, salt and sodium, not only for men and women but also for children.

The Food Standards Agency has introduced its own labelling system – 'traffic lights' – designed to provide similar dietary guidelines by drawing shoppers' attention to key points. 'Traffic light' information is displayed on the front of the pack. (See page 53 for more information.)

Most grocery chains and food makers, including Danone, Kellogg's, Kraft, Nestlé and PepsiCo, chose instead to develop their own front-of-pack labelling system, based on the GDA system.

UNDERSTANDING GUIDELINE DAILY AMOUNTS

Guideline daily amounts (GDAs) give a benchmark figure for Calories and key nutrients that a 'typical adult' should eat each day to maintain optimum health and weight. There may be separate charts for men and women or a single chart for 'adults'.

Where a single chart is used, the figures represent a woman's daily needs (energy intake for an average 'adult' is given as 2,000 Calories, for example). These figures are lower than for a man (average energy intake 2,500 Calories per day).

These figures are *average* daily energy needs for people of normal weight for their age who follow a moderately active lifestyle. But energy needs vary throughout life and according to circumstance. For example, you need fewer Calories, on average, if you want to lose weight and extra Calories if you are very active – doing manual work, sport, housework or DIY.

Energy Needs throughout Life

As you would expect, energy needs increase steadily throughout childhood. Boys aged four to six years need around 1,700 Calories. This rises to 2,000 Calories for seven- to 10-year-olds, and to 2,200 Calories for 11- to 14-year-olds. Girls need slightly less energy than boys, around 1,600 Calories from four to six years old, rising to 1,800 Calories for seven- to 10-year-olds, and 1,900 Calories from the ages of 11 to 14.

Adolescent males, aged 15 to 18 years, have the highest energy needs of anyone, at around 2,800 Calories. Energy needs then decline to around 2,500 Calories, on average, from ages 19 to 59. There is then a further decline to 2,400 Calories from 60 to 64 years, down to 2,300 Calories from 65 to 74 years and 2,100 Calories from 75 onwards.

Females aged 15 to 18 years have lower average energy needs than males of a similar age, at around 2,100 Calories. This falls to around 2,000 Calories between 19 and 50 years, 1,900 Calories from 51 to 74 years and 1,800 Calories from 75 onwards.

However, women need more Calories to cope with the energy demands of the last three months (third trimester) of pregnancy (an extra 200 Calories) and even more when breastfeeding (an extra 450 Calories plus).

ALPHABET SOUP

Confusingly, there are several nutritional guidelines currently in use by food makers and Government organisations. The Food Standards Agency uses 'dietary reference values' (DRVs), an umbrella term that covers 'reference nutrient intakes' (RNIs) and 'estimated average requirements' (EARs).

GDAs are based on DRVs but are not exactly the same. For example, the DRV for salt is 5g for women and 7g for men, but the GDA is set at 6g for both men and women.

DRVs were intended to replace an older system, 'recommended daily amounts' (RDAs). But RDAs are still used on labels for vitamins and minerals (see page 47).

Traffic Lights

The FSA's front-of-pack 'traffic light' system is intended to guide consumers on the fat, saturated fat, sugar and salt content of food products. The system doesn't just indicate how much of a particular nutrient a food product contains but also whether the content is high, medium or low, compared with official nutrition guidelines. The information is prominently displayed and colour-coded for easy reference.

The scheme took several years to devise and involved much consultation with scientists, nutritionists, government bodies and – crucially – supermarkets and food makers. The figure given is either 'per pack' or 'per serving'. For example, it might say 'fat – 21g per pack' or 'salt – 2g per serving'. The following colour codes are used:

* **Red** for high levels of fat, salt, sugar and so on
* **Amber** for medium levels
* **Green** for low levels.

The criteria for deciding what constitutes 'high', 'medium' and 'low' are based on UK and EC guidelines for healthy limits for the average adult. The code indicates whether a food is one that should be eaten on a regular basis (green), more sparingly (amber) or as an occasional treat (red).

Front-of-pack GDAs

The rival front-of-pack GDA system also uses colourful boxes for this information, but these boxes are not colour-coded. The GDA system shows the quantities of fats, sugar, salt and so on, just like the 'traffic light' system, but doesn't give a 'high', 'medium' or 'low' rating. It simply says what proportion of an adult's GDA this is. In effect, it takes information from the GDA box on the back and puts it on the front.

Shoppers must decide for themselves whether or not that figure is too high. Critics claim GDAs can be misleading. For example, the colours don't correspond to a code and so green may be used on a product that is high in fat or sugar. Also, the suggested serving sizes might be less than an average person would actually eat. If so, shoppers might be consuming more of a nutrient (fat, say) than the GDA figure suggests yet think they are keeping within the guidelines. The figure given may be for an adult when the product – such as breakfast cereal – might also be eaten by a child who has lower nutritional requirements and might eat too much.

Just how helpful it is to have two different front-of-pack systems is debatable. Not only are the two systems operating at the same time but they have also been inconsistently applied. For example, some brands display 'traffic light' information as horizontal bands; others show a series of boxes; and one has a 'colour wheel' like a pie cut in segments. This makes it more difficult to compare brands. Fortunately, shoppers can still use the nutritional information box to compare products.

CHECKOUT...

The nutritional information panel helps you compare brands on, for example, sugar, fat and salt content. The box also helps you plan a healthy diet for yourself and your family. As you read it, check:

* the 'per 100g' column to compare products
* the 'per serving' column to see how much fat, sugar and salt you'd actually eat
* the Calories (kcals) if watching your weight
* the dietary guidelines, such as traffic lights or GDAs, to follow a healthy diet
* the fibre content of starchy foods (aim for 2g or more per 100g)
* the saturated fat content (5g per 100g is a lot)
* the total fat content (20g per 100g is a lot)
* the added sugar content (15g per 100g is a lot)
* the salt content (1.5g per 100g is a lot).

See also ingredients (page 13) and food quality (page 57).

4

SIGNS OF QUALITY

All food products must satisfy minimum standards for food quality, as set by the Department for Environment, Food and Rural Affairs (DEFRA), the Food Standards Agency (FSA) and the European Commission (EC). This includes date marking, to ensure that food products offered for sale are good quality and safe to eat.

As foods often travel long distances to reach the shops, and face a wide range of temperatures and conditions en route, food makers have come up with new ways to extend their products' shelf life. Some well-established methods, such as freezing and canning, are accepted by shoppers, but some others are less popular. For example, many people think there is now too much plastic packaging, and treatments such as irradiation have been fiercely resisted by shoppers and consumer groups.

DATE MARKS – WHAT THEY MEAN

By law, pre-packed food must be date marked to show the maximum time allowed before a food product should be eaten (or disposed of, if uneaten). The date must be clearly shown and easily seen, on the most prominent side – usually the front – and not hidden by stickers. If there is too little space to display it there, the label must say where the date can be found (for example, 'For best before – see lid').

To avoid confusion, the date must be set out as: date/month/year, or date/month or month/year. If misreading a date carries a risk – for example, of thinking that '12/07' means December 2007 when it actually means 12 July – the month is written out in full or abbreviated (Jan, Feb and so on). There is much variation in the way the date is shown and whether the words 'use by' or 'best before' are actually used, or just the date itself displayed. The type and meaning of the date mark varies according to the product:

'USE BY'

The 'use by' date mark is found on pre-packed foods that quickly go bad and may be dangerous if eaten past their time. They include pre-packed uncooked meat and fish, ready meals, pastry products, sandwiches and some dairy foods. It is illegal for shops to sell or display food after its 'use by' date has expired. For example, 'use by 1 June' means *use by midnight* on 1 June.

The label usually says 'keep refrigerated' too, as most 'use by' products must be kept chilled. 'Use by' products often carry additional date information, such as 'once opened, consume within two days'.

Thorough cooking may extend the shelf life of foods beyond their 'use by' date. Freezing, soon after purchase, can prolong storage by a month or more. But, once defrosted, food must be cooked thoroughly and eaten promptly. Bear in mind that the quality of some foods, such as cheese, may be impaired by freezing, so check the label, which should say if a product is 'suitable for home freezing'.

Never eat refrigerated food after its 'use by' date has expired, even when unopened. Microbes may have built up to dangerous levels, no matter how fresh it looks or smells.

'BEST BEFORE'

The 'best before' date mark is found on longer-lasting pre-packed foods that decline in quality over time. The flavour, smell, appearance or texture might start to change after this date, for example. But the food may still be safe to eat for some time, provided it is stored correctly and the packaging is unopened and undamaged. (Eggs are an exception and must never be eaten after the 'best before' date – see page 69.)

The rules for 'best before' dates are:

* Foods with a shelf life of three months or less, such as bread and hard cheese, can display date and month only, although food makers can add the year if they wish.
* Foods with a shelf life of three to 18 months should display date, month and year.

* Foods with a very long shelf life, such as frozen and tinned products, can display 'best before end' and give month and year – or year only.

Storage information must be given as well. It is not illegal to sell food past its 'best before' date, provided it is fit to eat and of good quality (even if the packaging is a little worn), but you would expect to pay less. It must be made clear to shoppers that a product's 'best before' date is about to expire, so most shops set aside a separate 'reduced' section for such goods.

Tinned and Dried Food

Official guidelines say that even tinned and dried packet foods, and other products with a very long shelf life, should be consumed before – or soon after – their 'best before' date. It is a good idea to check the dates on tins and packets periodically (especially those that have got pushed to the back of the cupboard). You'll notice there is a wide variation in the length of 'best before' dates. Tins of soup, baked beans and tomatoes, for example, have a recommended shelf life of only two years, while some products are expected to last longer. Fish in oil has a 'best before' date of up to four years.

In practice, tinned and some packet food can last much longer than its 'best before' date and still be safe to eat – provided the container is undamaged. For safety, if you use tinned food much after the 'best before' date, heat it thoroughly before eating. This includes foods such as tinned fruit that you might normally eat cold. All tinned food has been pre-cooked to sterilise it, so five minutes' simmering should not alter the quality significantly. Never take risks with damaged packaging. If a packet is torn, smells mouldy or looks damp, or a tin is damaged or rusty it should be dumped (see box).

WARNING

Avoid buying damaged tins. If the inner coating or seals are damaged, acidic foods can corrode the metal, allowing air and germs to enter. This may happen to any tin over time, but especially to tomatoes or mandarins. Check your stock of tins periodically and use any that are approaching their 'best before' date. If a tin has gone rusty and/or is bulging (known as 'blown') don't open it and don't drop it. It may be under pressure from a build-up of gas from decaying food. Wrap it up and dispose of it carefully.

'SELL BY'
'DISPLAY UNTIL'

'Sell by' and 'display until' date marks are discretionary. They help shop staff manage stock control. It is not illegal for shops to sell food after its 'sell by' or 'display until' date has expired, provided the 'use by' date is still current. These dates may be useful to shoppers, helping you select the freshest items, but are no guarantee of quality.

EXCEPTIONS TO DATE MARKING

Exceptions to the date marking rules include fresh fruit and vegetables (provided they have not been peeled or cut into pieces), alcoholic drinks containing 10 per cent or more alcohol by volume, wines and some liqueurs, breads and bakery products normally eaten within 24 hours of being made, chewing gum (which is not regarded as an edible product as such), and very long-lasting products such as salt, sugar and vinegar.

STORAGE

Food labels must say if a product has special storage requirements, such as refrigeration or freezing, or has been treated to extend its shelf life.

REFRIGERATORS

The main storage compartment of the refrigerator keeps food fresh for a limited period only. The 'use by' date is the best guide to how long food will remain safe in the fridge. It is a good idea to use a fridge thermometer to check the temperature periodically. Bacteria thrive in temperatures from 5°C (41°F) and warmer (up to 60°C/140°F). So, ideally, your fridge should be no warmer than 4°C (34°F). Pack away shopping that needs to be kept chilled as soon as possible and leave food in the fridge until just before preparation, cooking or serving.

Refrigerators work best when well-stocked, otherwise each time the fridge is opened, cold air escapes and is replaced by warm air. At times of frequent use your fridge might not even reach its optimum temperature, and the food may be too warm for safety. One solution is to fill unused spaces with empty boxes, water bottles or storage containers. This limits the amount of cold air that can escape and ensures warm air that enters cools quickly. Leave a little space around food and containers to let the cold air circulate.

FREEZERS AND FREEZER COMPARTMENTS

You can extend the life of food by storing it in the frozen food compartment of a fridge or even longer in a freezer, if maintained at between −18°C (−1°F) and −22°C (−8°F). Use a freezer thermometer to check the temperature. Bacteria are not killed by freezing; they just go dormant. Once food has been defrosted it should be cooked and eaten or disposed of – never refreeze it.

The 'best before' date on frozen products only applies if the food has been stored at the correct temperature. Star markings on frozen food labels are used in conjunction with the stars shown on freezer compartments and freezers to indicate how long a product will stay edible and at what temperature. Freezer compartments marked with three stars or fewer are designed for pre-frozen foods only. Four-star freezer units (usually showing one star larger than the rest) will freeze non-frozen food from room temperature.

STAR MARKINGS

- No star: keeps pre-frozen and highly perishable foods for a few days only.
- * One star: keeps pre-frozen food for up to one week (–6°C).
- ** Two stars: keeps pre-frozen food for up to one month (–12°C).
- *** Three stars: keeps pre-frozen food for up to three months (–18°C).
- **** Four stars: keeps pre-frozen/non-pre-frozen food for up to six months (below –18°C).

BULK BUYING

If you buy frozen food in bulk to save money but only cook small quantities at a time, it is best to divide your purchases into smaller quantities and store in separate bags or boxes, clearly dated and labelled with cooking instructions. You then need remove only what you'll use without the risk of defrosting or contaminating the rest.

FRESH, FROZEN OR CANNED?

Frozen fruit and vegetables are frozen soon after picking and may be more nutritious than fresh produce transported long distances to reach the store. Fruit and vegetables to be tinned are cooked first, which depletes some vitamin C and folic acid content. Tinned food may be high in salt. In other respects, tinned produce is as nutritious as fresh food.

OTHER STORAGE INFORMATION

Treatments used to extend shelf life must be indicated on the label. Well-established methods include pasteurisation and ultra-heat treatment (UHT). Recent innovations include 'vacuum packing' and 'modified atmosphere packing' (MAP). All these methods inhibit bacteria and mould in chilled food products and extend shelf life beyond what can be achieved by chilling alone. (Milk labels must say if milk has *not* been heat-treated, as it may contain bacteria that pose a risk to health, especially for the young and old.)

Pasteurisation

Pasteurisation involves heating liquids to a high temperature well short of boiling to kill off bacteria without spoiling the flavour. This process is used to ensure milk is safe to drink and to extend the life of fruit juices and beer. Milk is heated to 63–66°C for 30 minutes or 72°C for 15 seconds. Other foods may be pasteurised at higher or lower temperatures. A little of the vitamin content may be lost as a result. Some nutritionists maintain that pasteurisation of fruit juice destroys enzymes that would otherwise promote absorption of nutrients.

Ultra-heat Treatment (UHT)

In this process, liquids such as milk are heated to well above boiling point (130°C) for a few seconds to extend shelf life almost indefinitely. This depletes the vitamin content more than pasteurisation and can alter the flavour.

— STAY FRESH —

The vitamin content of ready-prepared fruit and vegetables deteriorates rapidly during storage, even in a fridge. Aim to buy only as much as you think your family will eat over one or two days and restock as necessary. Better still, buy fresh produce – ideally from a trader who sources locally – and prepare it yourself as required.

Vacuum Packing

Vacuum packing involves removing all the air in the packaging. This keeps food fresh for longer and reduces the risk of bacterial contamination. It is used for bacon, cooked meat, pâté, ready-prepared vegetables, red meat and smoked fish. Vacuum-packed meat can look 'bleached' and sliced products become compressed and difficult to separate.

Modified Atmosphere Packing

Even in a refrigerator, many harmful bacteria thrive in natural air. There is less than 1 per cent carbon dioxide (CO_2) in natural air, and modified atmosphere packing involves increasing the CO_2 level by up to 30 per cent – at which most bacteria cannot survive. This method is now used for many difficult-to-store items including fresh pasta, prepared fruit and vegetables, red meat and ready meals.

Irradiation

Irradiation is a more controversial method of extending the shelf life of food products. Gamma rays, X-rays, electron beams or other forms of ionising radiation are passed through the food to kill insects, bacteria and mould, and inhibit sprouting and ripening that would otherwise shorten the shelf life. No radioactivity remains in the food, and changes are similar to those of pasteurisation. Irradiated food is not sterile and will not keep indefinitely so must be stored correctly.

STORING OLIVE OIL

Storage instructions on bottles of olive oil demonstrate why you should always read the label, even on commonplace products. The label advises you to store the oil in 'a cool, dark place away from direct sunlight', such as the bottom of the larder, and not to 'pour hot oil back into the bottle'. This is because good quality oil is squeezed out of the olives by 'cold pressing' – a process that minimises contact with air, heat and light. ('Extra virgin' olive oil is from the first pressing.) Unless stored correctly, oil combines with oxygen in the air (oxidation) to form unpleasant and potentially harmful by-products. However, the label will also say 'do not refrigerate'. This is because, if kept too cool – below 7°C (45°F), as in the fridge – the oil turns into a cloudy 'sludge' of oil crystals. If this happens the oil can be thawed gently without affecting the flavour.

Consumer groups have expressed concern that irradiation may be used to disguise unfit food that has started to decay. Bacteria would be destroyed but not necessarily the toxins they have produced and so could cause food poisoning. Currently, only dried herbs and spices are irradiated in the UK, but regulations allow other foods to be so treated, including cereals, fish, fruit, poultry, shellfish and vegetables.

FOOD STANDARDS

You can check the date marks, choose the freshest food available and make sure you store it correctly. But how do you know that the food you buy is good quality to start with? Most 'traditional' foods, such as bread, butter, cheese, eggs, milk, meat, jam and so on, are still made in ways that conform to strict rules. However, most foods today are not 'traditional' but made by industrial processes. Some have chemical additives and added water, starch and proteins, put there simply to bulk out the product.

In most cases, these 'additions' must be declared on the label. However, not all ingredients and processes have to be declared, and consumer groups and trading standards are recommending to the UK Government and EC legislators that such 'grey areas' of the law are tightened up. So how do you tell if a food is 'natural' or not?

In general terms, the more a food has been cooked, prepared or 'processed' in a factory, the more likely it is to contain additives and 'filler materials'. 'Formed' meats, for example, often used as sandwich fillers, are not pure pieces of ham, chicken or turkey, but may be bulked out with water, starch, sugar, salt and additives. This is discussed in more detail later in the chapter (see page 85).

EGGS

Egg labelling rules have changed in recent years. Eggs sold in shops and supermarkets are no longer labelled 'perchery', 'deep litter' or 'semi-intensive'. Now the terms 'organic', 'free range', 'barn' or 'caged' are allowed. The box and any extra packaging must include: 'best before' date, farming method, number and size (weight grade) of eggs, quality class, storage instructions and information such as country of origin and registered packing station number.

Storage Rules for Eggs

All eggs (and other raw chicken products) pose a risk from salmonella bacteria that can build up over time, so it is important to keep eggs cool (around 4–5°C/ 39–41°F) or as cool as possible if non-refrigerated. The label will state 'keep eggs refrigerated after purchase'. Eggs should never be eaten after their 'best before' date has expired. This date is set at a maximum of four weeks (28 days) after laying. But eggs can be sold up to three weeks (21 days) after laying, leaving you only a week before they must be consumed, so always check the date and buy the freshest.

Unless you use a lot of eggs each week, avoid bulk purchases and buy only what you need for the following week. If eggs are approaching their 'best before' date it is best to cook them thoroughly, such as by hard boiling or in a cake. Store eggs out of direct sunlight and avoid extremes of temperature. Avoid contact with strong odours and flavours such as garlic or onions, which can affect the taste.

Rearing Method

The box must say how the hens were reared:

* **Organic** (code 0) means free-range hens reared to the high standards set by the organic licensing body (see page 140).
* **Free range** (code 1) means the hens were allowed continuous daytime access to open air runs with vegetation such as pasture. Welfare standards are not as high as 'organic'.
* **Barn** (code 2) means the hens were stocked at a density of no more than nine per square metre and each bird had a minimum of 15cm perching available.
* **Caged** (code 3) means the eggs came from 'battery farms' in which the birds are kept in tightly packed conditions. Minimum welfare standards are laid down for these birds. If eggs carry the 'Lion' logo, the standards are higher (see box opposite).

THE 'LION' MARK

'Lion quality' is a scheme run by the British Egg Industry. The 'Lion' mark is seen on eggs from hens vaccinated against salmonella. A 'passport' system for flocks ensures the eggs are easily traceable. Eggs are packed, stored and transported under temperature-controlled conditions and carry a 'best before' date. The 'Lion' stamp is found on 85 per cent of eggs sold in the UK, including 'free range', 'barn', 'caged' and 'battery' eggs, and indicates a higher than minimum level of animal welfare. Some 10 per cent of the remainder are imported eggs, often produced in squalid conditions. An FSA study found salmonella contamination in 3 per cent of imported eggs.

Number and Size

The box must state the number of eggs (usually six or 12) and give the size or weight code. If there is a mixture of weight grades the box must say 'eggs of different sizes'. The size or size code indicates one of the following weights:

Size	Weight
Very large (XL)	73g or more
Large (L)	63–73g
Medium (M)	53–63g
Small (S)	less than 53g

Quality Class

Eggs can be graded A to C – but only 'Class A' can be sold in shops. 'Class A' shows the eggs have not been cleaned, refrigerated or preserved. If 'washed eggs' appears instead of 'Class A' it means the eggs are imported. Class B eggs may be suitable for domestic use but shouldn't be sold in shops. They may be sold direct to consumers from chicken farms or at farmers' markets (see below). Class B indicates they may have been cleaned, refrigerated or preserved. Class C eggs are used by the food industry only.

Direct Farm Sales

The rules for eggs sold directly from a farm or via farmers' markets, boot sales or door-to-door are slightly different. Farmers can sell their own ungraded eggs directly to the public for domestic use, provided the 'best before' date, storage information and code giving production site and farming method (0–3, as explained above) are displayed.

Other Information

There will be a code on the packaging that indicates the country the eggs came from ('UK' for United Kingdom and 'ES' for Spain, for example) and the number of the registered packing station. The name and address of the farm may be included, as well as other information such as how the chickens were fed ('corn fed'), breed of chicken, and possibly a packing or laying date. Promotional statements are allowed so long as they are not misleading.

BREAD AND FLOUR

There are strict controls governing the nutrient content and permitted additives used in bread and bread flour. Wholemeal flour must contain all the grain, including the fibrous outer coating, or bran, and the vitamin-packed wheat germ. The only additives allowed in flour are colouring, such as caramel (E150), and enzymes used to help bread rise. Most bread flour today is ground in roller mills to produce a fine texture. Stone-ground flour is milled the traditional way using millstones to produce a course texture. Bread freshly baked and sold on the premises doesn't have to be labelled, but most bread sold today is pre-packed so will have a name or description and ingredients list.

Types of Bread

The following are some of the most popular types of bread on sale today, together with any restrictions regarding how they are produced:

* **White bread** is made from flour that has been milled to remove most of the husk and wheat germ, and then bleached. At this stage the flour mostly contains just the starchy central section of the grain. Some fibre and wheat germ is put back to increase the fibre and nutrient content, and the bread is fortified with vitamins and minerals. White bread can contain additives, such as treatment and raising/improving

agents, and the preservative propionic acid to inhibit mould.

* **Brown bread** is similar to white bread in content in that it is made from flour from which 15 per cent of the bran and wheat germ has been removed. It is then coloured, usually with caramel. It must contain at least 0.6 per cent fibre.

* **Wholemeal bread** is the most nutritious as it retains most of the bran husk and wheat germ and so is high in fibre and nutrients. It may contain specified colouring such as caramel, and raising/improving agents, preservatives and so on, but you can also buy additive-free wholemeal bread. Bear in mind, though, that additive-free bread will not keep as long as other types.

* **Granary™ bread** is a form of brown bread made from special Granary™ flour, which contains coarse-ground ('kibbled') flour and whole grains. Granary™ bread may contain specified colouring, such as caramel, preservatives and other additives not allowed in wholemeal bread.

* **Gluten bread** has a high protein content (at least 16 per cent), especially of gluten. All bread contains gluten unless made with gluten-free flour. It is the protein content of flour that determines its strength. Traditionally, 'strong' flour is reserved for bread.

* **Wheat germ bread** is not the same as wholemeal. It is made with white or coloured flour,

and 10 per cent of processed wheat germ is added to the dry flour mix.

CHOCOLATE

Natural chocolate has proven health benefits. It is rich in antioxidants that help guard against heart disease, stroke and cancer. It also contains flavonols, plant chemicals also found in red wine, blueberries and green and black tea that relax the blood vessels, so improving blood flow and protecting against heart disease. Of course, there is a catch...

Chocolate contains cocoa butter, which is 60 per cent saturated fat and 40 per cent monounsaturated fat. In addition, many chocolate products are laden with corn syrup, hydrogenated fats and dairy fats – providing as much as 25 per cent of a woman's daily Calorie intake – and yet contain less than 20 per cent cocoa. The answer is to opt for products high in pure chocolate and low in added fats.

Chocolate is made from the seeds (not really 'beans') of the cocoa tree (the Latin name, *Theobroma*, means 'food of the gods'). These are pulped, fermented, roasted and ground to produce a chocolate 'liquor'. The cocoa butter is squeezed out to leave cocoa particles that are dried and ground into fine powder to make drinking cocoa.

Cocoa butter and/or cocoa are recombined and mixed with ingredients such as milk fat, sugar and vanilla, in various proportions, to create different types of chocolate. Lecithin (from soya) is added as an emulsifier to stop the cocoa butter separating and spreading over the surface to form a pale, greasy (but harmless) 'bloom'. This also happens if chocolate is not stored properly. There are three main types of chocolate:

* **Plain (dark or bitter) chocolate** contains 35–85 per cent cocoa solids, less than 12 per cent milk solids, lecithin (usually from soya), sugar and sometimes vanilla.
* **Milk chocolate** contains at least 25 per cent cocoa solids, 12–14 per cent milk solids and 3 per cent milk fat, plus additives, sugar and flavouring.
* **White chocolate** contains at least 20 per cent cocoa butter (but no cocoa), 14 per cent dry milk solids and 3.5 per cent milk fat, plus lecithin, sugar and vanilla.

COCOA ON PRESCRIPTION?

Doctors at the William Harvey Research Institute, London, believe dark chocolate is so beneficial that they have used it experimentally to treat heart patients. For optimal health benefits, you need just 25g of chocolate (containing 75 per cent cocoa solids) per day. Chocolate from Ecuador is the best, apparently.

DAIRY FOODS, FATS AND SPREADS

Milk, butter and other dairy foods are rich in vitamins, minerals and fatty acids. They can be high in fat, particularly saturated fat, and so it is best to eat full-fat types in moderation only and otherwise choose low-fat alternatives.

Butter, Margarine and Spreads

Natural butter can be good for you, provided it is not eaten in excess. It contains calcium and vitamins for strong bones, and short-chain fatty acids to help fight disease. Butter comprises 85 per cent fat and 15 per cent water. The fat is mostly saturated with some monounsaturated fat, and includes a little naturally occurring trans fat. The only permitted additives are salt and acidity regulators.

'Dairy spreads' may be sold as a spreadable alternative to butter, but cannot be called 'butter' as such. They usually contain a blend of cream or buttermilk and vegetable oil, plus colouring, emulsifiers, flavouring and salt.

Food makers provide a bewildering variety of 'healthy' margarines and spreads as alternatives to butter but some are not as 'healthy' as they seem. Hard margarines can have almost as much saturated fat as butter does. Low-fat spreads may be low in fat simply because they've been bulked out with water. So, when choosing a fat for spreading and cooking, always check the label to see what you are actually buying.

Margarine may contain processed vegetable oils, buttermilk and up to 16 per cent water. It must include added vitamins A and D to match those found naturally in butter. Low-fat spreads cannot be called 'margarine', and so often have their own brand name. They contain half the fat of margarine and more water. Like standard margarine, they are fortified with vitamins.

BUTTERCUP-COLOURED BUTTER

Traditionally, the colour of butter came from buttercups and other yellow flowers. As the cows grazed in the meadows, they ate the flowers that grew among the grass. The yellow carotene pigments in the flowers were stored in the cows' fat and from there passed into the milk, giving a creamy colour. The pigments got more concentrated as milk was churned into butter. Nowadays, most dairy herds spend little or no time grazing in fields and so yellow colouring is added to animal feed to get the same effect. As the colouring is not added to the butter itself it doesn't have to be declared on the packet.

Milk

Whole milk is a highly nutritious food, ideal for young children and active people – and much healthier than most highly processed sources of saturated fat. Adults whose diet is generally low in fat, especially saturated fat, have no reason to avoid whole milk either. If you need to limit your fat intake, skimmed and semi-skimmed milk are good alternatives. They have similar amounts of calcium and B vitamins, but less of the fat-soluble A and D vitamins. ('Enriched' low-fat milks have these vitamins added.)

Milk	Fat content (%)
Whole milk	3.8 (Channel Islands 4.8)
Semi-skimmed	1.5–1.8
Skimmed	0.1

Buttermilk

This is the milk residue left over from making butter, hence the name. It is added to many processed foods to add a creamy flavour. It contains some lactose (milk sugar), protein and minerals.

Cream

As with milk and butter, natural cream is good for you, provided it is eaten in moderation. It is easily digested, providing a quick energy boost; it strengthens bones and boosts the immune system. Different types of cream are distinguished by their fat content. Additives are strictly controlled. Unlike most cream, whipping cream has not been homogenised (that is, had the fat content dispersed as droplets in the water content) and so can be whipped. If it is pre-whipped it is called 'whipped cream'.

Type	Fat content (%)	Comments
Clotted cream	55	May contain the antibacterial nisin
Devonshire cream	55	
Double cream	48	
Tinned cream	35	May contain the antibacterial nisin
Whipped/whipping	35	May contain emulsifiers and stabilisers
Single cream	18	
Soured cream	18	Soured by rennet, acetic acid or lactic acid
Sterilised cream	18	May contain emulsifiers and stabilisers
Half cream	12	

Artificial cream is sometimes sold as a low-Calorie alternative to dairy cream. It is made from vegetable oils and water and may contain additives.

Ice Cream

Dairy ice cream is made with dairy fat, milk or cream and contains a minimum of 5 per cent milk fat. Non-dairy ice cream contains a minimum of 5 per cent vegetable oil – usually palm kernel oil – and will say 'vegetable fat' or 'non-milk fat' on the label.

Processed Cheese

Processed cheese, including cheese spread, is usually heat-treated to keep it fresh and contains additives such as emulsifiers to prevent the fat separating. It is often sold in silver foil or tubs and is very popular with children. Most types of processed cheese contain at least 50 per cent dry matter (calcium, protein and carbohydrate) and 40 per cent fat. The rest is water. Cheese spreads may have a higher water content.

FISH PRODUCTS

The amount of fish in fish products is set by law. For example, fish cakes, which are made with fish and potato, should contain at least 35 per cent fish. Fish paste should contain at least 70 per cent fish. Sirimi is a processed fish-based ingredient that can be flavoured and formed to make different products, such as 'crab sticks', which may not contain any crab meat at all. If sirimi has been used it must be declared.

If the label says a product is made from a particular fish species, such as cod or haddock, it must not contain any other type. But if the label simply says 'fish' or 'white fish' the food maker can legitimately use whatever fish stocks are available. The label doesn't even have to say what kind of fish has been used.

The method of processing, such as 'fillet', 'flaked', 'minced', 'shaped' or 'formed', must be declared on the label and, again, the terms must not mislead:

* **Shaped fillet** means a piece of fish is boned but otherwise left intact. It's then 'shaped' (cut) into fingers and, for example, coated with bread crumbs. The term 'shaped' should only be used for a fillet. You would expect to pay more for a fish fillet product.
* **Flaked and formed** has a clear meaning, too. Boned fish is made up of segments that separate easily into 'flakes' and can be 'formed' into fingers that retain some of the fillet texture. You would expect to pay less for a flaked fish product.
* **Minced and formed** means the fish is finely ground and 'formed' into fingers. This changes the texture of the fish but allows food makers to use more of the raw product. You would expect fish pieces made from minced fish to be the cheapest.

Food makers who use the term 'fillet' for fish fingers formed from flakes or minced fish risk being accused of a false trade description. The term 'minced fillet' is sometimes used but is meaningless.

You might expect a wide variation in price between top-of-the-range 'made with 100 per cent cod fillet' and bottom-of-the-range 'formed from minced fish', but this is not necessarily so. To decide whether you've had value for money, compare the price, quality and ingredients with the food makers' description.

HOW MUCH FISH?

The contents of fish products can vary widely from that shown on the label. In a Bucks County Council Trading Standards survey of bread-crumbed fish products, such as fish fingers, one brand contained 14 per cent *less* fish than indicated on the label, while another had 13 per cent *more* fish than stated. Of 30 leading brands analysed, eight were deficient in fish content. If you feel you have been misled by the labelling on a fish product, contact your local trading standards department for advice.

FRUIT DRINKS

Different rules apply to fruit drinks depending on whether they are called a 'crush', 'juice', 'nectar' or 'squash'. The accurate name (also known as its 'legal' name – see page 101) may not be immediately apparent, so don't be misled by 'marketing' titles such as 'orange zest', 'juice burst' or 'sunshine delight', which have no legal meaning. According to the law, it is up to consumers to read the whole label – including the small print – before buying.

Freshly squeezed juice is the most natural product. It has all the flavour and vitamins of the fruit it came from, provided it is kept in the fridge and drunk soon after purchase. Concentrated fruit juice is made by evaporating up to 50 per cent of its water in order to reduce its volume and so cut transport costs. Once the juice reaches its destination it is reconstituted and

Type of drink/Comments
Fruit crush, ready to drink
Contains 5 per cent minimum fruit
May contain artificial sweetener

Fruit juice/pure juice, ready to drink
May contain added sugar (up to 15g per litre)
Orange juice may contain added sulphur dioxide
   (up to 10mg per litre)
Pineapple juice may contain dimethylpolysiloxane
   (anti-foaming agent)

Fruit nectar, ready to drink
Contains 25–50 per cent fruit juice and may
   contain colourings

Fruit squash, dilute first
Contains 25 per cent fruit (citrus) or 10 per cent
   fruit (other flavours)
May contain added sugar or sweetener
May contain colourings

Sweetened fruit juice, ready to drink
Contains added sugar (more than 15g per litre)

Fizzy juice/nectar, ready to drink
Must be labelled 'carbonated' if carbon dioxide
   (CO_2) level exceeds 2g per litre

bottled or packaged for sale. There may be a slight reduction in flavour and vitamin content but the juice has a longer shelf life. It must say on the label 'from concentrate'. Heat treatment (see page 65) extends the shelf life even more.

If there is more than 15 per cent added sugar the label must state 'sweetened' and give the maximum amount present. However, a juice product can contain up to 15 per cent added sugar and still say 'unsweet-ened' on the label.

JAM AND MARMALADE

The minimum amount of fruit and added sugar in jam and other preserves is set by law. Bear in mind that sugar is a natural preservative. Low-sugar or no-added-sugar types will not keep as long and so must be refrigerated after opening.

MEAT

The label on a 'composite' meat product – that is, a food item such as sausage that contains meat along with a mixture of other ingredients – must show just how much meat went into it. However, the rules governing what can legally be described as 'meat' changed substantially in 2003 when the UK came into line with other EU countries. These rules do not apply to raw cuts of meat, such as chicken breast or pork loin, to which nothing has been added (other than tenderising enzymes) and which should contain nothing but meat. But if a piece of meat contains

Preserve	Fruit content (%)	Comments
Extra jam	up to 40	*60 per cent added sugar*
Jam	35	*60 per cent added sugar* *May contain undeclared sulphur dioxide*
Reduced-sugar jam	35	*30–55 per cent added sugar* *Refrigerate after opening*
No-added-sugar jam	35	*Added fruit juice (e.g. grape juice)* *Refrigerate after opening*
Marmalade	27.5 citrus fruit/peel	*60 per cent added sugar*
Reduced-sugar marmalade	27.5 citrus fruit/peel	*30–35 per cent added sugar* *Refrigerate after opening*

anything extra, such as added water, starch or protein, it becomes a 'meat product', not a raw cut of meat.

The Old Rules

Previously, UK food makers had to give the quantity of meat in their products – not the percentage. The definition of 'meat' was 'flesh including fat and skin, rind, gristle and sinew in amounts normally associated with the flesh used'. 'Rind, gristle and sinew' are collectively known as connective tissue. No limits were set on the amount of skin and connective tissue, other than that they were in amounts 'normally associated', which was open to interpretation.

The term 'meat' could include offal, such as heart, kidney and liver; 'head meat', including tongue; and mechanically recovered meat (see box, page 89), which could be reformed to look like natural meat. There was a legal minimum regarding the amount of 'lean meat… free of visible fat' that could be used in a meat product.

The New Rules

Now the food label must say what *proportion* of the product is meat (expressed as a percentage) but not the *quantity*. The way this is worked out is rather complicated and varies according to the meat product. The definition of the term 'meat' has also changed and now refers to 'skeletal muscle' – that is the larger areas of flesh actually used to propel the animal, such as breast and leg meat on chicken and turkey, and the legs and flanks on pigs, cattle and sheep.

The new definition still allows 'naturally included or adherent fat and connective tissue' to count as 'meat' (whether or not it gets separated in cooking), but there are now strict limits on how much there should be. These limits vary, according to animal and product, but are based on what consumers might reasonably expect to find in a piece of raw meat. For example, fatty meats, such as pork, beef and lamb, can include more fat than lean 'white' meat such as chicken and turkey. The maximum amounts allowed for the most popular types of meat are:

Meat	Fat (%)	Connective tissue (%)
Pork	30	25
Beef	25	25
Lamb	25	25
Chicken	15	10
Rabbit	15	10
Turkey	15	10

Although labels on composite meat products no longer have to state the quantity of meat in the product, they must give the meat content as a *percentage of the weight of the whole product*. As with other products, this applies to the key ingredients. In a chicken pie, for example, the key ingredient is chicken. So, if a 100g portion of 'chicken in bread crumbs' contains 65g chicken, the label will state: 'chicken (65%)'.

MECHANICALLY RECOVERED MEAT

Mechanically recovered meat (MRM) must now be listed separately. The label must also say the type of meat ('mechanically recovered pork' or 'mechanically recovered chicken', for example). Mechanical recovery of meat (or 'mechanically separated meat') uses high-pressure machines to extract the tiniest scraps of flesh, fat and sinew from the bone after the bulk of the meat has been removed in other ways. This means more of the protein is recovered and makes each carcass more profitable but substantially alters the texture of the meat extracted – sometimes described as a meat 'purée' or 'slurry'. There is no evidence that it is harmful, but many shoppers choose to avoid it.

MRM can be reformed to look like individual chunks of meat, or made into fancy shapes and coated in bread crumbs to appeal to children. It cannot be included in the total percentage of meat shown on the label. For example, a chicken product might state 'chicken (45%), and mechanically recovered chicken'.

There is a difference between MRM and mechanical de-boning, in which powered cutting devices are used to remove large chunks of meat. In this case the muscle has the normal appearance of meat. It can be kept intact or minced, as required. Meat removed in this way counts towards the total percentage of meat given on the packet. The fact that the meat was obtained by 'mechanical de-boning' does not have to be stated.

This must include no more than the maximum amount of fat and connective tissue allowed for whatever type of meat it is. In the case of chicken this is a maximum of 15 per cent fat and 10 per cent connective tissue. Additional fat and connective tissue in the product must be listed separately, although food makers do not have to give a percentage for this.

Offal, 'head meat', tongue and mechanically recovered meat cannot count towards the 'meat' content but must be listed separately by name, as, for example, 'beef heart', 'lamb's liver', 'pig's kidney', 'pork head meat' or 'mechanically recovered chicken'.

Food makers don't have to give the percentage of offal unless it is a key ingredient, such as kidney in a 'steak and kidney pie'. In that case it might say, for example, 'kidney (10%)'. Products derived from meat, such as gelatine, stock and fat added on its own, do not count as 'meat' either and must be listed separately.

Combining Meat

In the case of products that include more than one species of animal, all the meat from a single species can be added together and listed in the ingredients – for example, as 'pork (15%), beef (10%)'. That percentage must include no more than the limits allowed for fat and connective tissue (see above). Again, any added fat and tissue must be listed separately. This is particularly important for products such as sausages that can include a high proportion of fat and connective tissue.

For products containing cooked meat, such as a

pizza topping, the percentage given is the amount of cooked meat, so the limits on fat and connective tissue don't apply. If any fat has separated during cooking it can't be included in the percentage.

Traditional Products

Some traditional meat products, such as burgers and pies, are covered by special rules. For example, a meat pie weighing more than 200g must contain at least 12.5 per cent meat, whether pork, beef or chicken (see chart below). Food makers can include more meat if they choose. The following are the minimum proportions of meat allowed in some traditional meat products:

Meat product	Minimum meat content (%)
Burgers	
– pork	67
– beef	62
– chicken	55
Burgers (economy)	
– pork	50
– beef	47
– chicken	41
Chopped	
– pork	75
– beef/lamb	70
– pork luncheon meat	67
– chicken	62

Meat pies	
chicken/pork/beef (200g+)	12.5
chicken/pork/beef (100–200g)	11
chicken/pork/beef (under 100g)	10
Mixed pies	
beef & potato/chicken & leek	7
steak & kidney pudding	7

Added Meat

Labels on tins of corned beef say that the product contains '120 per cent' meat. This sounds absurd. After all, how can you end up with more meat than you started with? The reason is that some water is lost during cooking or processing (drying, for instance) and this lost weight must be allowed for. So food makers start off with 120g of meat to end up with 100g of final product – hence 120 per cent.

Hidden Ingredients

So, do the new laws ensure that consumers will know exactly what has gone into the meat they are buying? Not entirely... and this is where it gets more complicated. Food technology allows every scrap of protein to be extracted from an animal and put to work to increase the weight of a piece of meat. Added animal proteins, and vegetable proteins from milk, cereals and soya, can be used as 'binders' to enhance its flavour and texture. They not only help bind meat and fat but also increase water retention.

Starch and/or vegetable protein and/or animal protein from the same animal species can legally be added to meat products that *look like* a 'cut, joint, slice or portion' of meat – *without being included in the name of the food*, provided they are added for a 'technological purpose' only. For example:

* Protein from chicken skin and bones can be added to a cut of chicken.
* Cow blood can be added to roast beef.
* Pork protein from pork skin and bones can be added to ham.

In all these cases, if the added protein is from the same species it does not need to be included in the product name. The term 'technological purpose' is not defined but, according to FSA guidelines, should not be used as a meat extender (or replacer) to bulk out the meat content. The Trading Standards Institute (TSI) calls this a potential 'rogue's charter'. The TSI believes it gives less-reputable companies an unfair advantage over firms that produce good-quality meat products. Some food technology companies claim they can, for example, double the weight of a piece of ham simply by adding water, and so boost profits for food makers considerably. The TSI and the FSA are pressing for tougher rules on meat labelling and the issue is now being examined by the EC.

┌─────────────────────── **DRAGON AND MASH** ─┐

Black Mountains Smokery was told to rename their 'Welsh Dragon' sausages after Powys Trading Standards pointed out this was a false trade description. They contained no actual dragon meat.

└──┘

Added Water

Added water in raw meat must be declared in the ingredients if it is more than 5 per cent above what would be present naturally or exceeds 5 per cent of the finished product – but the ingredients don't have to state how much more. However, it cannot be sold as fresh meat but becomes a 'meat preparation or meat product' that must be labelled to say that water has been added. As ingredients are listed in descending order of weight and the percentage of meat must be shown, you may be able to work out indirectly how much added water is present.

Uncooked bacon and other raw cured meat can contain up to 10 per cent water without it being declared. This is the minimum amount of water needed in the 'wet cure' process mainly used today. Where bacon contains more than 10 per cent, the name must include a statement, 'with added water' – but still needn't say how much.

— WITH ADDED CHICKEN... —

Shropshire Trading Standards has reported the case of a food maker who produced a 'chicken sandwich' in which only 80 per cent of the 'chicken' was *real chicken* – the rest was added water, additives, protein and starch. Such practices are not illegal so long as the required information is printed on the label. But responsible food makers may soon have to use the term 'real chicken' to distinguish it from the other kinds.

Foreign Proteins

If protein comes from a different species it must be stated in the name. For example, if 'beef plasma' (cow blood) is added to chicken breast (yes, it does happen) the product must be called 'chicken breast with added beef protein'. It is illegal to add undeclared 'foreign animal protein' just to increase water content. But new processing methods make it hard for trading standards to identify when 'foreign proteins' have been added.

Special Rules

* Uncooked meat products must not contain brain, feet, lung, oesophagus, rectum, spinal cord, spleen, stomach, testicle and udder, but large and small intestine can be used to provide the skin for raw sausages, black pudding and haggis.
* The laws regarding chicken and other poultry allow some water to be included without being

declared if it is 'extraneous' – that is, absorbed naturally during plucking, washing and cooling. This does not include water added as an ingredient.

* Where a meat product includes meat 'on the bone', such as a roast chicken wing or a lamb chop, the bone is included in the weight – and hence percentage – in the ingredients. This is

---

KOSHER AND HALAL MEAT

Strict adherents to the Muslim and Jewish faiths must eat food prepared in a way that conforms to their religious principles. Muslim food is known as 'halal', which means 'lawful' in Arabic. Jewish food is 'kosher', from the Hebrew word meaning 'proper'.

Jewish and Muslim religious laws dictate which types of meat can be eaten – pork, for example, is prohibited in both religions. Blood is regarded as unclean and so halal animals are slaughtered in a ritual way and the carcass hung long enough for all the blood to drain out. Abattoir staff must be of the correct faith and use religious words.

The terms 'kosher' and 'halal' do not have strict meanings under UK food laws. Nevertheless, if meat or other food is falsely labelled 'kosher' or 'halal' the distributors and/or sellers can be prosecuted. Trading standards officers have prosecuted food importers who labelled chicken breast containing pork protein as 'halal'.

because the law assumes that shoppers expect it and allow for it. It is important to take any bone into account when buying a meat product.

ESTIMATED CONTENTS

Along with the issue of quality comes that of quantity – have you got everything you've paid for? This seems straightforward at first, but food makers can mislead without actually breaking the law. Food labels must display the average weight or volume. If there is an 'e' after the figure it means that the weight is an estimate. This might apply to loose or mixed ingredients where it would be impossible to make every packet the same weight. That estimate should be close, however, or the food maker risks a fine.

You could compare the estimated contents of a product with rival brands – one product may seem like a bargain when actually it just contains less of the food, even though the packaging may appear the same size.

Some food makers have been known to reduce the quantity yet charge the same price. This is not new. Tales of chocolate bars that steadily shrink while the wrapper stays the same size are legendary. Consumer groups who monitor these changes have found several brands that have been reduced in quantity without an equivalent (or any) price reduction – in effect, a stealth price rise. These include:

Product	Down from	to	Reduction (%)
Baked beans	450g	420g	(↓30)
Chocolate bar	7 (pieces)	6 (pieces)	(↓14)
Chocolate drink	400g	300g	(↓25)
Chocolates	11 (pieces)	10 (pieces)	(↓9)
Crisps	200g	170g	(↓15)
Mints	226g	200g	(↓11.5)
Sausages	475g	400g	(↓16)

On one occasion the reason quoted in the press was to 'improve' the product in line with Government healthy-eating guidelines. The new product was lighter and had less fat and fewer Calories. This does not explain why there was no equivalent price reduction.

CHECKOUT...

Pre-packed foods have to follow strict rules on safety and quality. However, food makers have many ways to cut costs, prolong shelf life and maintain product quality. Whether you approve of them all is a matter of preference, but knowing what is involved helps you make informed choices. Check:

* the 'use by' date to see how long foods with a short shelf life stay safe to eat
* the 'best before' date to see how long products with a long shelf life stay safe to eat and of good quality
* 'star markings' to see how long frozen foods should be kept
* whether the product has been concentrated, heat treated, irradiated and so on – these processes may affect flavour and vitamin content
* the codes on egg boxes
* the meat content on meat products to see if you're getting what you expect
* the estimated contents – weight or volume – and compare against other brands to make sure you are getting what you pay for.

See also ingredients (page 13) and nutritional information (page 27).

5

WHAT IT SAYS
AND WHAT IT MEANS

Food makers go to great pains to promote their wares. The name is chosen to be exciting or inviting. The packaging is decorated with eye-catching colours and patterns or mouth-watering images, and covered with promotional claims that suggest loving care or generations of expertise have gone into the product. Here, we look at the facts behind the embellishments.

WHAT'S IN A NAME?

Where will you find the *legal name* of a food product? That is, the name that explains what a food product really is, according to law, rather than what the food maker has chosen to call it. Will you find the legal name in the most prominent position, in large letters so that it can be seen clearly? Not necessarily. It could be anywhere. What may look like the name can quite legitimately be total hype:

> **Tangy Fruit Flavour Burst Delight**
> **– with added additives!**

That is the brand, marketing or 'fancy' name. It needn't even be a helpful description, so long as it doesn't actually mislead. The legal name, or legal description, '*fruit flavour drink*', may be printed underneath or in tiny letters on the back. Is this legal? Well, yes. Food makers can put a meaningless name on the front provided the legal name is somewhere on the label. Shoppers are expected to study all the writing on the packaging to find out just what they're buying.

FRUIT OR JUICE?

Northamptonshire County Council Trading Standards Service took Purity Soft Drinks to court over a product named 'Juice Burst', alleging false trade description as the drink contained only a tiny amount of fruit juice. Trading Standards lost at magistrates' court on the grounds that the word 'burst' qualified the word 'juice', in effect rendering it meaningless. They also lost on appeal (*Lewin v Purity Soft Drinks 2004*). Mr Justice Field said, 'It is the expectation of consumers that the label should be read as a whole.' In other words, so long as the legal name is printed on the label, no matter how hard it is to find, consumers aren't being misled. 'The test is not what reasonable consumers *would* think, it is what reasonable consumers *could* think.'

PRECISE NAME

Nevertheless, as far as the legal name is concerned, food makers can't choose words just because they sound good to the marketing department. There are rules governing how foods should be named and described. In general, a legal name must be precise enough to indicate its true nature and distinguish it from foods it might be confused with.

In some cases the content of a product is quite clear. If a label says 'carrots', there's little doubt what's on offer. But if processing is involved, this must be included in the legal name or description, no matter how simple. This is especially important where processing affects the flavour, colour, texture, cooking method or storage qualities.

For example, products that have been pickled, smoked, salted, dry-roasted, dried, ultra heat-treated, pasteurised, concentrated, condensed, frozen and so on must say so – prominently. If a food is artificially sweetened, it must display 'with sweeteners' next to the name. The legal name must also reflect any changes to the processing, recipe or ingredients that might affect the final product, if customers could be misled.

If a product is new, or the 'fancy name' doesn't fully explain what it is, there must also be a description giving all relevant information. For example, a product called 'Prune and Custard Delight' might be described as a 'prune dessert with custard topping'. Some product names have a legal definition. These include fruit, sugar, wholemeal bread and yoghurt.

Fruit and veg may need to include the variety ('honey-dew melon', 'Jersey Royal potatoes' and so on).

Some food names are not defined in law yet are established by custom and practice. Customers know what to expect when they see 'muesli' or 'pizza' on a label, for example, and would feel cheated if they got something else. They would be entitled to pop along to their local trading standards department, who might decide to take the matter further.

Words used must describe the product accurately and be unambiguous. There is a distinction, for example, between fish smoked in the traditional way, in a smoke house, and fish treated with a solution that imparts an artificial 'smoked' colour and flavour.

If a name is well established it need not be literally true – but it must not mislead. For example, a cottage pie must contain beef, unless labelled as a vegetarian alternative, in which case the name must include the main ingredient (such as soya or Quorn™). Similarly, if pre-packed meat is frozen and then defrosted just before sale the label should say so clearly. But there are subtleties that may trick the unwary...

FLAVOUR OR FLAVOURED?

Foods marked 'flavoured' must contain the product named. For example, the flavour of a 'strawberry flavoured' product must come from strawberries (although the amount may be small). But foods marked 'flavour', as in 'strawberry flavour' jellies, can contain artificial strawberry flavouring only (plus sweeteners and colourings). You have to check the list of ingredients to be sure.

HEDGEHOG LITE

Pub landlord Philip Lewis got so fed up with customers asking for 'hedgehog flavoured crisps' as a joke that he made some. However, his crisps were actually flavoured with pork fat, so he fell foul of food labelling laws. Once he put 'hedgehog flavour crisps' on the packet he was able to keep within the rules.

REGIONAL NAMES

Product names that include a country, region, town and so on may not necessarily come from there. A name could simply indicate a food style, like French mustard. You wouldn't expect a Swiss roll to come from Switzerland, especially as we are the only ones to use the name (Americans call it a 'jelly roll'), nor a Bakewell tart to come from Bakewell.

Even the more authentic 'Bakewell pudding' (made by two different bakeries, both claiming to have the 'original recipe') could be made in Buxton, but if there was a risk that consumers might be misled, thinking they'd bought traditional 'Bakewell pudding' from Bakewell, the label would have to make it clear exactly where it was made.

This issue can throw up curious anomalies, however. The famous 'Melton Mowbray' pies need not hail from Melton Mowbray, but they must be made in Leicestershire! Northern Foods wanted to make them outside the county, but the courts took a different view. Some regions have exclusive rights to their products that are protected within the EC. For example, Champagne can only come from the Champagne region of France. But even here there are exceptions. Because of a legal loophole, US wine-makers can call their equivalent fizzy beverage 'champagne' too – only with a small 'c'.

HOW REAL IS REAL?

The word 'real' doesn't necessarily mean natural ingredients were used. Some products marked 'real orange flavour' or 'real meat juice flavour' can be made with artificial flavourings only. Check the ingredients list to see if the 'real' product is actually there.

BEWARE HONEYED WORDS

Wording such as 'tender', 'juicy' and 'succulent' may be included but is largely irrelevant, designed to draw your eye away from key words. You might find the term 'with added succulence' on meat products, yet all this means is 'with added water'. If you see 'tender', 'juicy' or 'succulent' on a label, ask yourself – compared with what? Would food makers claim some of their other products were 'tough', 'stringy' and 'tasteless'? Of course not. That shows how meaningless these terms are.

So it is important to ignore the hyperbole and focus on the key words. If a label says 'tender pieces of fish in a delicious crunchy coating', ask yourself why it does not specify 'cod', say, or 'haddock'. Perhaps it's a species you've never heard of (and wouldn't like to meet on a dark night). If it says 'chocolate flavour sponge delight', ponder why it's not called 'chocolate cake'. Perhaps because there's no 'true' chocolate in it.

PROMOTIONAL CLAIMS

Firms that make unsubstantiated or false claims can fall foul of laws on food labelling, composition and manufacture. These laws also apply to food sold loose, such as bakery and delicatessen products, if any claims on nearby stickers clearly refer to items on sale. Many promotional claims, such as 'fresh', 'traditional' and 'home-made', do not have legal meanings, but the food makers must still ensure shoppers are not misled.

Illustrations count too. A picture of raspberries on a product made with artificial flavourings would be misleading. Nevertheless, you may find labels illustrating foods not contained in the product with the words 'serving suggestion' nearby (often in small letters) to avoid claims of misrepresentation.

Here are some common promotional claims, along with guideline definitions:

'AUTHENTIC'

'Authentic' describes a product that follows a well-established recipe and/or is produced in a geographical region closely linked with that product. It helps to distinguish a product with a long history from more recent variations – especially ones that differ in flavour, strength, appearance or nutritional value. For example, 'authentic' applied to Wensleydale cheese might be acceptable if a product was made in that region of Yorkshire using a well-established recipe and production process.

'EXTRA FRUIT'

Terms such as 'extra fruit' could be misleading because they beg the question: compared with what? If the label makes this claim, the total amount of fruit included must be shown as well. You can then compare the figure given with similar products to see if they really do give you extra.

'FARMHOUSE'

'Farmhouse' means the product was made in a kitchen on a *working* farm. It could be an extension from the kitchen, built to make food products commercially. But if the extension grew too large, or was separated from the kitchen, the term would be misleading. 'Farmhouse' also implies hand-prepared, traditional cooking methods, and fresh farm ingredients sourced locally. Food processing and cooking equipment should be typical of a farmhouse, such as mixers, blenders and ovens. Industrial-scale equipment would be unacceptable.

👁 **WATCH OUT FOR...** 'Country-style', in a similar context. This is meaningless so ignore it.

'FREE RANGE' / 'BARN'

'Free range' means that farm animals, such as chickens, turkeys and pigs, get continuous daytime access to an outside run where they can forage among pasture. It ensures more freedom of movement and fresh air than other forms of rearing. Free-range egg-laying chickens, for example, must have at least four square metres of space and be kept at a maximum density of no more than 2,500 per hectare. Their sheds must comply with EC requirements regarding the welfare of laying hens. However, the sheds may be so large that the chickens rarely venture outside. 'Organic free-range' animals are guaranteed to have spent time outside in a natural environment. All companies producing 'organic' foods must have been certified by a legally recognised authority (see page 70).

FREE RANGE CHAMPIONS

Food products marked with the 'V' logo may contain eggs and egg-derived products (such as albumen) from battery farm chickens. The Vegetarian Society, however, *only* endorses products containing eggs *if they are free range* (see also page 140).

'Barn', in the context of eggs, indicates that hens have room to move around, with access to perches, nest-boxes and litter. Conditions are more humane than for 'caged hens' as the animals can forage and roost (see page 70). Animal welfare group Compassion in World Farming regards both 'barn' and basic 'free range' conditions unacceptable and only recommends 'organic free range' foods.

> 👁 **WATCH OUT FOR...** 'Farm fresh' and 'country fresh', often applied to battery-farmed animals. The term 'carefully managed' means nothing, so ignore it.

'FRESH'

'Fresh' is applied to foods with a limited shelf life sold shortly after catching, harvesting, butchering or processing. It includes food chilled (to just above or below 0°C), chopped, pasteurised (for safety reasons), trimmed or washed, but not tinned, cooked, dried, frozen, salted, smoked, vacuum packed or chemically processed to extend its shelf life.

The terms 'fresh-cooked', 'fresh-baked', 'fresh-picked', 'freshly prepared' and 'freshly squeezed' are valid only if a timescale is given (for example, 'fresh-cooked this morning'). If it says 'fresh-baked in store', check whether the product was part-cooked elsewhere and finished off in the shop's own oven.

> 👁 **WATCH OUT FOR...** 'Fresh-tasting' – this just means 'tangy'.

'FRUIT JUICE' / 'JUICE DRINK'

A product labelled 'fruit juice' must contain 100 per cent fruit juice. If made from fruit juice concentrate it must say so in the name (such as 'orange juice – made from concentrate'). A product labelled 'juice drink' can legally contain only low levels of 'pure' fruit and include added sugar and artificial flavourings, sweeteners and colourings to make up the difference. Look at the ingredients list to see how much fruit the drink provides – it should be given as a percentage. Or check to see where it is in the ingredients list – the further down the fruit appears the less there is.

'HOME-MADE'

This shows a product has been made in a domestic kitchen or a commercial building that is as close to a domestic kitchen as is practicable. It implies traditional methods, using raw ingredients prepared by hand from scratch – with the possible exception of ingredients such as stock cubes, pickles and jams that might be found in any domestic kitchen. Food processing and cooking equipment, such as mixers, blenders and ovens, should be of a typical kitchen type. Industrial-scale equipment would be unacceptable.

👁 **WATCH OUT FOR...** Factory-made products illustrated with domestic kitchen scenes.

'NATURAL'

Strictly speaking, 'natural' describes individual or

single-ingredient foods that have not been altered in a way that changes their flavour, colour or shelf life – other than by long-established methods, such as baking, blanching, roasting, freezing, fermenting, pasteurising, wood smoking and jam making. Butter, cream, traditional cheeses, yoghurt, jam, marmalade and smoked fish and meats can be described as 'natural' if customary methods of cooking, fermentation, flavouring, smoking or washing were used. Products that include non-traditional flavouring, or are bleached, concentrated, pasteurised, sterilised, smoked or tenderised using chemicals, are not 'natural'.

Similarly, a flavouring derived from a single source using methods such as crushing, distillation or solvent extraction is 'natural'. A flavouring that has been extensively processed or includes additives – even 'natural' ones – is not 'natural'. Processed foods containing a mixture of ingredients are not 'natural' as such but the label can say they are made with 'natural ingredients' if the individual foods that go to make up the whole product are 'natural', as defined here.

👁 **WATCH OUT FOR...** 'Natural' when it just means 'unflavoured'.

'ORIGINAL'

'Original' means that a well-established product, recipe or process was the first of its kind on the market, or the first one produced by a food maker. It might distinguish the first (and most popular) brand from other products made by a food maker. To claim a product is 'original', food makers must keep the same recipe and production methods. However, if only the processing changes the label can claim to follow an 'original recipe'. And if only the recipe changes it can claim to be 'made the original way'.

👁 **WATCH OUT FOR...** 'Original' when it just means 'unflavoured'.

'PURE'

The term 'pure' should be used for individual products or ingredients that have had minimal processing and no added flavourings, including sugar and preservatives. For example, traditional jams and marmalades can claim to be made with 'pure fruit' if they contain traditional ingredients such as pectin, but not preservatives such as sulphur dioxide. Fruit juices can be 'pure' if they include added water, but not added sugar or citric or ascorbic acid. If a label says 'pure ingredients', all the ingredients must comply with these guidelines.

👁 **WATCH OUT FOR...** 'Pure' when it just means 'unflavoured'.

'-STYLE'

Adding the word '-style' to a food claim can be misleading unless referring to a recognised cuisine.

'Provençal-style' might be okay if used to indicate herbs and spices traditionally used in that region, but terms such as 'traditional-style' are meaningless.

'TRADITIONAL'

'Traditional' describes a recipe, cooking process or method of rearing or production with a very long history – decades at least. Unlike 'original' (see page 112), 'traditional' should not be used just to distinguish one recipe or method from more recent varieties, unless they are also well established. It is okay to say a product is made from a 'traditional recipe' if the production process has changed, or made using 'traditional methods' if the recipe has changed, but the distinction must be clear.

> 👁 **WATCH OUT FOR...** 'Traditional' when it just means 'plain'.

TERMS WITHOUT AGREED MEANINGS

Many terms used on labels have no agreed definitions and so are virtually meaningless. The FSA hopes to issue guidelines for all these terms, following consultation with the various interested parties concerned.

* **Economy** usually means a basic 'no-frills' standard at a cheaper price, or in a larger 'bulk' size that – weight for weight – works out cheaper than a similar quantity of a standard-size product.
* **Luxury** should imply quality but often indicates

a high price and may mean a product is high in fat (from cream or vegetable oil) or sugar.

* **Value** usually means a basic standard at a lower price than similar products in the range, or a lower price than competitors are offering.

As there is no agreed meaning for these terms, the only option is to compare price and ingredients with similar products. Look at the quantities of main ingredients, especially the more expensive ones such as meat, fish, fruit and nuts, and compare them with similar products. Check whether specific ingredients, such as 'beef', 'kidney', 'cod', 'walnuts' or 'cherries', have been listed, or whether food makers are using generic terms such as 'meat', 'white fish', 'mixed nuts' or 'mixed fruit'. If so, they may have cut corners and you must then decide whether the product is worth buying.

Other terms with no agreed meaning include: 'garden fresh', 'good for you', 'healthy', 'natural goodness', 'wholesome goodness', 'nutritious', 'ocean fresh' and 'oven fresh'. Ignore them.

CHECKOUT...

The marketing departments of food makers work hard to present their products in the best possible light. The name given to a product and the way it is described must not give a false impression but shoppers can easily be misled unless they know the potential pitfalls. When studying the label, check:

* if the name really describes the product; if not, look for the real name or description – it may be hidden away
* the name against the ingredients list and make sure the product is correctly described – it is an offence for food makers to give a misleading impression
* the name and/or ingredients list to see whether the actual product is there or just its 'flavour'
* the ingredients list to see if named foods have been given or just generic terms such as 'fish', 'mixed fruit' or 'mixed nuts'
* the promotional claims – be dubious about any that can't be justified.

See also ingredients (page 13) and health claims (page 117).

6

MAKING
HEALTH CLAIMS

Increasingly, many food makers are promoting products as having extra health-giving, body-and-brain-boosting nutrients, and fewer unhealthy, fattening, blood pressure-raising ingredients. Some health claims are legally defined. Others are covered by official guidelines designed to keep food makers on the right side of the law.

COMMON HEALTH CLAIMS

Many food labels make claims such as 'fat free', 'less than 5 per cent fat', 'low sugar', 'low fat', 'no added sugar', 'reduced fat', 'reduced sugar', 'high fibre'. These products may well aid a healthy lifestyle but shoppers must take care: products that claim to be, for example, 'low in fat' may be high in sugar or salt, so always check the nutritional information box. This information must be included if the product makes a health claim.

False claims are illegal. For example, a label should not state that a food has 'special qualities', such as being 'high in vitamins and minerals', when all similar foods have similar qualities.

'LIGHT' / 'LITE'

The terms 'light' and 'lite' have no legal or generally agreed definition and can be ambiguous. 'Light' might apply to the level of fat, overall Calories or even the food's texture. A food might be 'light' only in comparison with other products made by the same firm – not other brands. Look at the nutritional information box and compare the product with others to establish whether the claim of 'light' is valid.

'FREE FROM'

The term 'free from' may be used misleadingly, especially where a food substance would never be present in the first place. For example, vegetable oils can be marked 'cholesterol-free', yet cholesterol only occurs naturally in some animal products, never vegetable-derived ingredients. Also, a label can say – quite legally – that a product is 'free from' a substance even though there may be some residue. For example, an 'alcohol-free' product can legally contain up to 0.05 per cent alcohol. This may be of concern to people who want to avoid alcohol for moral, health or religious reasons.

'REDUCED LACTOSE'

Lactose is the sugar found naturally in milk. People

who are lactose intolerant lack the enzyme to digest lactose and suffer symptoms (see page 190) unless they consume foods with little or no lactose. The FSA recommends that 'reduced lactose' products should have at least 25 per cent less lactose than standard milk products. However, this may not be enough to prevent symptoms. Unless a label gives a percentage reduction, the product should be avoided by people who are lactose intolerant.

'SUITABLE FOR DIABETICS'

Foods targeted at diabetic people may have the words 'diabetic' or 'suitable for diabetics' on the label. These products are marketed as being healthy, yet 'diabetic' foods may be high in fat. They can include sweets, biscuits and cakes that should be eaten sparingly and not play a significant part in a healthy diet. 'Diabetic' foods are more expensive than standard sugar-free and reduced-sugar versions. People with diabetes eat similar foods to anyone else, so the concept of 'diabetic' food is out of date. The FSA is lobbying Government and EC legislators to put an end to the use of these terms on food labels.

'HEALTHY EATING'

Ready meals, such as curries, pasta dishes and traditional foods like shepherd's pie, that are labelled 'healthy eating' meals may be lower in fat or Calories simply because they are smaller portions of standard high-fat meals. They may even be high in other ingredients you are trying to avoid, such as salt. Check the 'per 100g' section of the nutritional panel and the serving size against similar products.

'10 PER CENT MORE!'
'5 PER CENT LESS!'

Food makers often use percentages to show how much extra 'goodness' has been added, or how much of an unwanted ingredient has been taken out. An extra 10 per cent of fish may sound a lot, but if there was only 5g previously, for example, this adds only an extra half a gram. Similarly, a '5 per cent' reduction in sugar or salt can still leave the product with unacceptably high levels. For example, 1.25g of salt per 100g is a lot of salt. A 5 per cent reduction would bring it down to 1.175g – which is still too much salt! Check the ingredients to see how much there is.

'95 PER CENT FAT-FREE!'

This means the product contains no more than 5g fat per 100g of product, which is high compared with a 'fat-free product' (less than 0.15g fat per 100g) or a 'low-fat' product (less than 3g fat per 100g).

HEALTH CLAIMS –
WHAT THEY SHOULD MEAN

Here are some common health claims and official guideline definitions for these nutrients, now standardised throughout the EC:

FIBRE

Claim	*Per 100g/100ml*
'High fibre'	over 6g fibre
'Source of fibre'	over 3g fibre

FAT

Claim	*Per 100g/100ml*
'Fat-free'	under 0.15g fat
'Less than 5 per cent fat'	under 5g fat
'95 per cent fat-free'	5g fat
'Low fat'	under 3g fat
'Low in saturates'	under 1.5g saturated fat
'Reduced fat'	25 per cent less fat than standard product
'20 per cent less fat'	20 per cent less fat than standard product
'Low cholesterol'	under 20mg cholesterol

SUGAR

Claim	*Per 100g/100ml*
'Sugar-free'	under 0.5g sugar
'Low sugar'	under 5g sugar
'No added sugar'	none added (may contain natural sugar, from fruit)

SALT

Claim	*Per 100g/100ml*
'Low sodium'	under 0.12g (120mg) sodium
'Low salt'	under 0.25g salt

👁 **WATCH OUT FOR...** 'Controlled salt', which is meaningless. The term has been used on the labels of some of the saltiest bread-crumbed fish products around.

CALORIES

Claim	*Per 100g/100ml*
'Low Calorie'	under 40 Calories per 100g
'Reduced Calorie'	25 per cent fewer Calories than standard product

---

THAT'S CHEATING!

Calorie information is useful if you are following a Calorie-controlled diet. Low-Calorie or reduced-Calorie foods help with a weight-loss diet only if you eat the right amount. Take care not to compensate by eating more of a 'low-Calorie' product than you should or you'll still be consuming excess Calories.

'RICH SOURCE OF VITAMINS'

There are 13 commonly recognised vitamins: A, C, D, E, H and K plus the seven B vitamins – B1, B2, B3, B5, B6, B9 and B12. Most natural ingredients contain vitamins in their unprocessed state but levels vary depending on when and where the food was grown. Food makers can replace vitamins lost during storage and processing to restore the content to average natural levels. But they can't claim a food has been 'fortified' with vitamins if it only contains as much as you'd expect normally.

Food makers can make special health claims about the following vitamins only: A, B1 (thiamin), B2 (riboflavin), B3 (niacin), B9 (folic acid) and B12 (cobalamin). All other vitamins can be mentioned only in the ingredients list, nutritional panel or product name (for example, if it is a vitamin supplement). To do so elsewhere is to make a 'health claim' and is illegal.

National guidelines set average levels for vitamins that most adults should obtain from the diet. These are called the 'recommended daily amount' (RDA). To justify a health claim, a normal serving must provide the average adult with at least one-sixth (17 per cent) of their RDA of that vitamin. To claim a product is a 'rich source' it must contain at least half (50 per cent) of the RDA of that vitamin (see page 48).

'FUNCTIONAL' FOODS

For decades, food makers have added special ingredients to boost the 'health-giving' properties of their products. Breakfast cereals, margarines and bread have long been 'fortified' with vitamins and minerals, and table salt contains iodine to prevent goitre (swelling of the throat due to an enlarged thyroid gland, often caused by iodine deficiency). The major change in recent years is the much wider range of products that claim these 'health-giving' benefits. A product that has been enhanced to function as a special health food is called a 'functional food'.

The Japanese led the way with 'functional' biscuits, cheese, cocoa, confectionery, milk, soft drinks, spreads, tea and yoghurt. In the UK, 'prebiotic' and 'probiotic' yoghurts have been joined by omega-3s, dairy peptides and plant sterols/stanols. In some cases the health claims made for these foods are proven. In other cases, however, there is a fierce debate among the scientific community as to just how beneficial they are.

Some 'functional' products also come laden with less-welcome ingredients such as excess sugar, salt and fat. They are often much more expensive than their 'non-functional' equivalents, too. In addition, the benefits of some 'functional' ingredients can be obtained just as easily by following a balanced diet containing 'natural' ingredients – that is, foods that have received little or no processing. Nevertheless, many people feel better for eating functional foods and so, for them, the extra cost is a price worth paying.

DAIRY PEPTIDES

Dairy peptides are 'mini proteins'. They are made by using enzymes to break down casein, a milk protein (hence the name 'dairy' peptides). Dairy peptides occur naturally in some cheeses, but in amounts too small for a beneficial effect. In higher doses they reduce mild hypertension (raised blood pressure). They do this by blocking an enzyme that would otherwise cause blood vessels to narrow and so raise blood pressure. As the dairy peptides cause blood vessels to widen, blood pressure falls.

Hypertension is a risk factor in heart disease, stroke and kidney disease. Even a small drop in blood pressure can go some way to reduce this risk. Dairy peptides are added to drinks for use mainly by people who are already trying to manage high blood pressure through diet and exercise. If you are taking medication, ask your doctor before using dairy peptide-fortified food.

OMEGA-3 ('FISH') OILS

Omega-3s are a family of polyunsaturated fatty acids. Their unique structure makes them essential for the retina, brain and nerves in developing babies. The human body can't make omega-3s so we have to get them from our food (or mum's food, in the case of developing babies), hence they're called 'essential fatty acids'.

Omega-3s are often called 'fish oils' but this is a misnomer as they also come from plants. Alpha-linolenic acid (ALA), for example, is found in green leafy vegetables, linseeds, rapeseed oil, soya oil and walnuts. The most important omega-3s for humans are eicospentaenoic acid (EPA) and docosahexaenoic acid (DHA). The body can make these from ALA, but not efficiently. Omega-3s are also found in lamb and beef and in butter from grass-fed cows, but the best source is oily fish.

Health benefits claimed for omega-3s include

protection against heart disease and stroke, reduced pain and stiffness in rheumatoid arthritis, relief of symptoms of Alzheimer's disease, and improved concentration, memory and behaviour in children. Ideally, you should consume an average of 450mg of omega-3s per day (about 3,000mg per week). You can get all the EPA and DHA you need from oily fish. Two portions of tinned salmon, or a tuna steak, contain around 3,000mg of omega-3s, and a mackerel portion has 4,500mg.

Omega-3s are added to 'functional foods', too, including cereal bars, bread, eggs, juice, milk, tinned pasta and yoghurt. In most of these cases the omega-3 is added to the product after processing. An exception, however, is eggs – the hens are fed on seeds rich in omega-3 fatty acids. Two medium eggs contain over half the recommended daily intake of omega-3s.

The amount of omega-3s contained in other products varies, however, so check the nutritional information box to ensure they provide enough for your dietary needs. If the label does not say 'fish' or 'fish oils' or 'EPA and DHA', the omega-3 probably comes from plant ALAs. (If you have a fish allergy you should choose ALA products.)

Some omega-3 products are high in fats and sugar, so study the label before buying.

MILK MARKETING

One dairy producer had to change the marketing campaign it was running for a brand of 'clever milk' containing added omega-3s. The campaign was based around scientific studies that suggest omega-3s may play a role in enhancing learning and concentration in children. However, those studies involved a mixture of nutrients and larger doses of omega-3 than are available from functional milk. To get the equivalent intake of omega-3, children would need to drink 5 litres of 'clever milk' a day. There is no suggestion here that the producer had set out to mislead consumers but it shows how careful food makers must be in the claims they make for their products.

PROBIOTIC FOODS

Some 95 per cent of the cells in the human body are bacteria and only 5 per cent are human. A scary thought. Luckily for us, bacteria are very small. In the intestine they make up a whopping 1kg of our weight – equivalent to a bag of sugar. Most gut inhabitants are harmless. Some, like *Lactobacilli* and *Bifidobacteria* are beneficial. Others, like *Escherichia coli*, *Clostridium*, *Campylobacter* and the yeast *Candida albicans* are harmful. It seems to make sense to try to tip the balance by eating foods containing beneficial bacteria.

The benefits of a thriving population of 'gut flora' are numerous. Friendly bacteria keep disease-causing microbes in check, boost the immune system, help guard against cancer, manufacture vitamins, produce up to 10 per cent of our energy, and may even reduce cholesterol.

THE FIRST PROBIOTIC

The benefits of yoghurt came to world attention early in the last century, thanks to the work of a Russian scientist, Elie Metchnikoff. He studied a group of Bulgarian mountain peasants and claimed their life-long good health was due to daily yoghurt consumption. Dr Minoru Shirota of Japan heard of this and isolated a strain of beneficial gut bacteria, which he named *Lactobacillus casei Shirota*. He added it to a milk drink that he gave patients at his health clinic. He later went on to found the Yakult company.

Bacteria used to make yoghurt are not very hardy and many are killed by stomach acids, bile salts and enzymes on their way to the bowel. Probiotic species are tougher, either occurring naturally or having been specially bred. Look for the words 'live' and 'active' on the label and choose brands that name the organism, such as *Lactobaccillus*, *Lactococcus* or *Bifidobacterium*. Some products contain a probiotic yeast, *Saccharomyces*. Probiotic yoghurts can be high in added sugar (especially fructose – see page 21) to counteract the sour taste of the lactic acid they contain, so check the label and choose those with the least sugar. You could add a little fruit to sweeten them.

PRO- AND ANTIBIOTICS

Probiotic foods are best avoided when taking antibiotics. Most of the friendly bacteria in the food will be destroyed, and there is a slight risk that any survivors will develop antibiotic resistance which they then pass on to disease organisms. Probiotic foods are ideal once you've finished taking antibiotics, however. They provide an easily digestible source of energy and help replace gut bacteria killed by the medication.

PREBIOTIC FOODS

As well as consuming probiotic bacteria, you can eat special food to ensure the good bugs grow and thrive. That's the principle of *pre*biotic food. Friendly bacteria live on a special type of fibre made up of short chains of simple sugars, called oligosaccharides. This is indigestible to harmful bacteria, which lack the enzymes to break it down. It passes through to the bowel enabling good bacteria to thrive and multiply. There are several kinds of prebiotic:

* fructo-oligosaccharide (FOS) found in artichokes, asparagus, bananas, barley, chicory, corn, garlic, leeks, oats, olives, onion, peas and whole wheat

* galacto-oligosaccharide (GOS) found in milk (especially breast milk) and soya
* inulin, found especially in chicory
* lactulose, which is a laxative (in large quantities).

We can get 2–3g of prebiotics from the diet but for maximum benefit we need at least 5g daily. Now food makers are adding *pre*biotics to *pro*biotic yoghurts, bread, breakfast cereals, fruit and cereal bars, chocolate spread, drinks, margarine, salad dressing and supplements. Some of these are low in prebiotics but high in sugar and fat, so study the nutritional information carefully before buying.

PLANT STEROLS AND STANOLS

Sterols and stanols are plant extracts that lock onto cholesterol in the bile salts secreted into the gut, and stop it being reabsorbed. The liver must then take cholesterol from the blood to replace what is lost, so reducing blood cholesterol levels. Sterols and stanols occur naturally in cereal foods, cooking oils, fruits, nuts, seeds and vegetables – but in modest amounts. Now food makers add them to drinks and spreads.

These foods may lower moderately raised levels of blood cholesterol, when used as part of a lifestyle that includes a healthy diet and regular exercise. But if you are taking cholesterol-lowering drugs you should seek your doctor's advice before trying them. They are unsuitable for pregnant/breastfeeding women, or children under five.

HEALTHY? PROVE IT!

New EC rules will make it much harder for food makers to print health claims on food labels. Once the rules have been fully implemented, all health claims must be scrutinised by the European Food Safety Authority and only those judged to be scientifically credible will be allowed. Health claims will not be allowed for foods high in fat, sugar or salt.

CHECKOUT...

Many food labels boast about their health benefits, but are they justified or just snake oil? Rule makers are getting much tougher on what can and can't be claimed about food products so, when studying the label, check:

* health claims against the nutritional panel and make sure the claims hold true
* you are getting all the vitamins, minerals, fibre or essential oils the label claims
* you are not being bamboozled by percentages, such as '95 per cent fat-free'
* the evidence given for health-promoting claims (such as lowering cholesterol) – contact the food maker and ask for proof
* with your doctor or other healthcare worker if you are taking medication that may conflict with a health-promoting food ingredient.

See also Chapter 5.

7

HOW ALCOHOLIC IS IT?

The alcohol content of a drink is given as 'percentage alcohol by volume' and is shown on the label as '%ABV'. This is useful when comparing products, such as two brands of beer, but not so helpful in telling you exactly how much alcohol there is in the glass of wine, beer or spirit you would actually drink. What you really want to know is how many units of alcohol you would be consuming if you bought one brand or type of drink instead of another. This is important for health reasons, so that you do not drink more than is good for you; and also for legal reasons, so that, for example, you do not risk losing your driving licence.

Just choosing a slightly larger wine glass can make a surprisingly big difference to your alcohol intake. Wine is traditionally served in 125ml or 175ml glasses. The difference between the two can add an extra half a unit or more per glass. Many pubs and bars now serve wine in even larger glasses – up to 250ml – which is double the volume (and double the units) of a standard 125ml glass. The wine glasses you use at home may not be a standard measure so it is worth checking exactly how much they hold by filling with water and then emptying into a measuring jug.

CONVERTING %ABV TO UNITS

You can convert %ABV to units using a calculator. Multiply the volume of the glass by the '%ABV' marked on the can or bottle and divide by 1,000. For example, a 125ml glass of Bordeaux (12.5 per cent ABV) contains 125 x 12.5/1000 = 1.56, or just over 1½ units.

The Department of Health's recommended maximum daily alcohol intake is four units for men and three units for women, but you should also allow two or three alcohol-free days each week to give the liver time to recover. Of course, this doesn't apply to drinking and driving. If you are unsure how many drinks you can consume without exceeding the legal limit it is best to avoid all alcohol if you are driving.

Some alcoholic drinks give the number of units per glass, but most don't. The charts opposite can help you calculate the number of units in:

* a standard 125ml glass of wine or fortified wine, ranging from 10–18 per cent ABV
* a large 175ml glass of wine, fortified wine or vermouth, ranging from 10–18 per cent ABV
* a standard 500ml can of beer, ranging from 3.5–5 per cent ABV

* a standard 25ml measure of spirits, ranging from 35–40 per cent ABV.

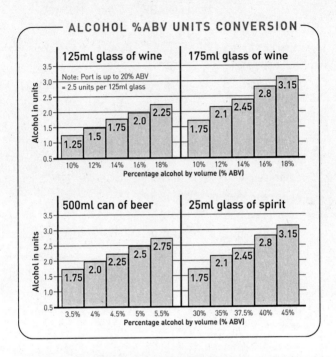

ALCOHOL %ABV UNITS CONVERSION

ALCOHOL CONTENT OF POPULAR BEVERAGES

Over the page are some popular alcoholic drinks with their '%ABV' and units equivalent:

	% alcohol by volume (ABV)	Units per glass (125ml)	(175ml)
Sparkling wine	5.5–12.5	0.7–1.6	0.97–2.2
Kabinett	9.0	1.0	1.6
Piesporter	9.0	1.0	1.6
Liebfraumilch	9.0–11.0	1.0–1.4	1.6–1.9
Riesling	9.0–12.0	1.0–1.5	1.6–2.0
Cava	11.5	1.4	2.0
Muscadet	12.0	1.5	2.0
Champagne	12.0–12.5	1.5	2.2
Bordeaux (claret)	12.0–13.5	1.5–1.7	2–2.4
Sauvignon Blanc	12.0–13.5	1.5–1.7	2–2.4
Chianti Classico	12.5–13.0	1.6	2.2–2.3
White Burgundy	12.5–13.0	1.6	2.2–2.3
Chablis	12.5–13.0	1.6	2.2–2.3
Chardonnay	12.5–14.0	1.6–1.8	2.2–2.5
Red Burgundy	13.0	1:6	2.3
Merlot	13.0–14.0	1.6–1.8	2.3–2.5
Gewürtztraminer	13.0–14.0	1.6–1.8	2.3–2.5
Shiraz	13.0–14.5	1.6–1.8	2.3–2.5
Cabernet Sauvignon	13.5–14.0	1.7–1.8	2.4–2.5
Vermouth	14.7–15.0	1.8–1.9	2.5–2.6
Sherry	15.0–17.5	1.9–2	2.6–3.0
Port	19.0–20.0	2.4–2.5	2.4–3.5

	% alcohol by volume (ABV)	Units per glass (500ml)
Bitter	3.0–5.0	1.5–2.5
Lager	3.5–5.2	1.75–2.6
Cider	4.2–7.5	2.0–3.8

	% alcohol by volume (ABV)	Units per glass (25ml)
Cognac	36.0–40.0	0.9–1.0
Rum	37.5	0.9
Vodka	37.5–40.0	0.9–1.0
Gin	37.5–43.0	0.9–1.0
Whisky	40.0–45.8	1.0–1.2

CHECKOUT...

Alcohol is one of life's pleasures and has proven health benefits, in moderation. But excess alcohol puts your health – and possibly driving licence – at risk, so make sure you know how much you are drinking. When buying alcohol, check:

* the size of your drinking glasses with a measuring jug
* the percentage alcohol by volume (%ABV) listing on the label and compare with similar drinks or brands
* how much you actually drink by converting percentage alcohol to units
* that you don't exceed your maximum daily limit – four units or fewer for a man and three units or fewer for a woman.

8

PROUD TO BE 'GREEN'

Many food labels highlight a product's 'green' credentials regarding animal welfare, fair trade and environmental sustainability. The question is, can you trust these claims? A label may imply a 'green' image by, for example, using green ink or pictures of plants and wildlife. If the label includes a recognised logo and/or wording representing an 'accreditation body' it usually indicates that the product lives up to its claim. Without such an indication, however, any claim should be treated with suspicion.

A GUIDE TO 'GREEN' CLAIMS

Food makers must be able to justify 'green' claims. It is an offence to mislead. If in doubt, contact the company and ask for evidence. There should be a contact address or advice line number on the label. If you think you've been misled, contact your local authority trading standards department. The following is a guide to some of the organisations whose job it is to ensure that 'green' claims are valid.

EUROPEAN ECO-LABEL

The EC is attempting to standardise products making a 'green' claim under its 'eco-label logo'. This is a green flower made up of a blue ring of stars surrounding an 'E' symbol. There will also be a unique identification code. The 'eco-label logo' indicates that a food was produced using methods that meet EC criteria designed to reduce the harmful impact that farming had previously on the environment. To qualify, a food firm must be independently assessed by a government body. In the UK, this is the Department for Environment, Food and Rural Affairs (DEFRA).

ORGANIC FOOD

The word 'organic' indicates that a food was produced using methods certified by the UK Register of Organic Food Standards (UKROFS) or by a body approved by them, such as Organic Farmers & Growers. Perhaps the best-known certifying body is the Soil Association, set up in 1946, which sets the Soil Association Organic Standards.

Organic farming methods restrict the use of artificial chemical fertilisers and pesticides. As a last resort only, farmers can use one of seven approved pesticides. Livestock are reared without the routine use of drugs, antibiotics and wormers. To avoid a build-up of parasites, pests and disease, livestock are regularly moved to fresh pasture, plant crops grown on a piece of land are changed annually, land is left fallow (unused) some years and/or the land is used for grazing instead of crops.

It is illegal to claim a food is organic unless it has the 'organic certification' number prominently displayed on the packaging ('Organic Certification UK2', for example). Firms using an organic certification label must expect both annual inspections and random spot checks, which in some cases involve removal of soil and other samples for laboratory analysis. Checks are carried out on arable farms, livestock and horticultural establishments, food processors, retailers, wholesalers, importers and even abattoirs.

Organic food tends to be more expensive than non-organic produce. But supporters claim it is healthier, tastier and has less environmental impact. Organic farms have higher animal welfare standards than other establishments (including non-organic 'free-range' farms) and a greater abundance and diversity of wildlife. Because of a shortage of UK-grown organic food, some organic foods come by air. If this concerns you, look on the label for 'country of origin' and choose UK foods, or buy from outlets that source locally.

As some ingredients are not available in organic form, it may not always be possible to make a product '100 per cent organic'. But a label can say 'organic' if 95 per cent of the ingredients were produced organically and the other 5 per cent are from an approved list. Cornflour is allowed as a 'non-organic agricultural ingredient', for example.

A product containing less than 95 per cent organic ingredients cannot be labelled 'organic'. However, it can say 'made with organic ingredients' if 70 per cent of ingredients are organic and the other 30 per cent are 'approved'.

Individual ingredients may be listed as organic (for example, 'organic pears') or marked with an asterisk or other mark, with a footnote stating '[*] indicates organically produced ingredient' or '[*] ingredient produced to the UK standards for organic farming' or similar. The method of organic production must be displayed, such as 'organically grown' (if it is a plant crop), 'organically reared' (if it is a food animal) or 'organically produced' (if it is a food product, such as milk or cheese).

Non-pre-packed fruit and vegetables are not labelled 'organic' as such but are usually sold in a separate 'organic' section of the store. However, all other rules on organic production must be applied.

ASSURED FOOD SCHEMES

A logo depicting a red tractor is found on products from farms and other establishments that follow rules laid down by Assured Food Standards. AFS represents the interests of groups including the British Retail Consortium, Dairy UK, the Meat and Livestock Commission, the National Farmers' Union and the Ulster Farmers' Union. It sets the standards and manages the bodies that police them. Independent assessors conduct regular inspections regarding animal welfare (including transportation); food safety; hygiene; concern for the environment; crop production; feed supplies; abattoirs and meat processing.

The welfare standards set by AFS are not as strict as those for organic certification, and some AFS farms use intensive methods. However, as this is a voluntary scheme, shoppers know that AFS members have chosen to follow higher-than-minimum standards. Such schemes are open to European producers, too, if they meet the required standards. An AFS logo with a Union flag means food was produced, processed and packed in the UK.

INTEGRATED FARM MANAGEMENT

Integrated farm management (IFM) is regarded as a 'halfway house' between organic and intensive farming. It combines traditional farming with modern technology to offer profitable farm production with reduced environmental impact. The green 'LEAF' logo can be found on some foods produced using IFM methods. 'LEAF' stands for Linking Environment and Farming, an organisation formed in 1991 by farmers, agricultural groups, environmentalists, consumer groups, supermarkets, academics and government officials.

IFM farms minimise pesticide use through natural pest control, such as by leaving some land uncultivated to allow predatory birds and beetles to thrive. There is a greater abundance and diversity of wild plants and animals than on intensive farms. IFM criteria, however, are not as strict as those for organic farms.

'FREEDOM' FOOD

The blue 'flying F' Freedom Food logo is found on products made from animals reared according to standards set by the Royal Society for the Prevention of Cruelty to Animals (RSPCA). Freedom Food is a non-profit organisation set up by the RSPCA in 1994. It includes small-scale, large-scale, indoor and outdoor farm systems within its remit, as well as abattoirs, animal hauliers and meat-processing companies.

To qualify, firms must comply with Freedom Food welfare standards, including annual inspections and spot checks by RSPCA officials to ensure they are following the rules. The RSPCA also carries out 'traceability' checks on food products carrying the logo to ensure that everyone in the supply chain is a member. Freedom Foods are not necessarily free-range products but do indicate a reasonable level of animal welfare.

VEGETARIAN AND VEGAN FOOD

The 'V' logo indicates that a product *must* be suitable for vegetarians and *may* be suitable for vegans. The logo is voluntary. Many supermarkets use their own 'V' symbol but the strictest criteria are applied by the Vegetarian and Vegan Societies.

Vegans do not eat any animal-derived foods. Vegetarians do not eat foods that cause the death of any animal. This includes cochineal, a colouring made from beetles, and animal rennet – an enzyme used to make cheese – if it comes from the stomachs of slaughtered cows and calves. Even animal-derived ingredients that are only used for processing and not present in the final product (such as fish isinglass and gelatine) are regarded as unacceptable. Vegetarians do eat some foods derived from live animals, such as eggs, milk, cream, cheese made using vegetarian rennet, honey, pollen, beeswax and yoghurt (made with vegetarian gelatine).

There is no legal definition of 'vegetarian' or 'vegan' but food makers who knowingly use unsuitable ingredients in vegetarian products can be prosecuted. Food makers must also take care to ensure vegetarian foods are not accidentally contaminated with animal-derived ingredients. However, some animal-based ingredients need not be listed if they make up less than 2 per cent of the final product.

Checklist of Animal Ingredients

If you follow a vegetarian or vegan diet, always check the ingredients. The following are some of the most common animal-derived ingredients:

* albumen and lecithin from eggs
* aspic, gelatine, glycerine (or glycerol) and rennet from animals
* casein, lactitol, lactose and whey from milk
* cochineal and shellac from insects
* chitin from shellfish.

Vegetable forms and alternatives are available for many 'animal' ingredients and may be listed as such. For example, glycerine/glycerol can be made from fermented sugar; lecithin usually comes from soya; rennet used in vegetarian cheese is made with bacterial or yeast enzymes; and agar, carrageen and gelozone are non-animal alternatives to gelatine. Suet may be of animal or vegetable origin.

EGG NOGGIN

Wine, beer, cider and spirit labels need not state if animal products were used. In addition to fish isinglass and gelatine, animal ingredients used in alcoholic drinks include albumen and lysozym from egg, and casein and whey from milk.

'FAIRTRADE' GOODS

The 'Fairtrade' logo is found on foods made with produce from Third World farmers and growers who receive a price set by the certifying authority, Fairtrade Labelling Organisation International (FLO-Cert). The best-known 'Fairtrade' products are probably tea, coffee, bananas and chocolate, but there are many others. The price the consumer pays covers the cost of sustainable production and includes a premium to help fund environmental, social and economic development projects in the Third World.

Fairtrade products can cost as much as 50 per cent more than equivalent brands. It has been claimed that supermarkets earn more from Fairtrade goods than from equivalent brands. However, a spokeswoman for a leading grocery chain said Fairtrade goods are often 'quality products' and, like all products, are priced 'as competitively as possible'. What is undeniable is that many Third World producers wouldn't be able to negotiate a viable price for their goods without 'Fairtrade' – earning up to six times as much as they would do otherwise.

SUSTAINABLE FISH PRODUCTS

Many people are concerned about the use of intensive fishing methods, the depletion of fish stocks and the effect on coastal communities that rely on fishing to survive. Such concerns led to the establishment of the Marine Stewardship Council (MSC). The council's blue logo can be found on seafood products that come from well-managed fisheries. MSC was set up in 1997 by the Worldwide Fund for Nature (WWF) in conjunction with Unilever, then the world's biggest buyer of seafood, as a global, non-profit organisation. In 1999, MSC became independent, funded by charities and corporations. MSC also runs campaigns such as the 'Fish & Kids' project, to promote sustainable (MSC-labelled) seafood in schools and family restaurants.

RECYCLED OR RECYCLABLE?

A logo showing arrows in a stylised circle or triangle means the packaging material is recyclable – that is, can be reused, or recycled, into another product – or has already been made from recycled material. If it is recyclable, it should say what it was made from ('aluminium', for example). Your local authority can tell you where and how to recycle it. If made from recycled material, the logo should say how much ('Made from 80 per cent recycled paper', for example), so you can tell how 'environmentally friendly' it is.

Some products are now made of 'biodegradable' packaging. This quickly breaks down into simple compounds that enter the natural decay cycle and do not persist in the environment. The label should state which part of the packaging is biodegradable and how long it takes to break down. Contact the packager if these details are not shown. One supermarket chain has introduced 'compostable' packaging, made from maize, sugar or plant-based starch. This is placed in a compost bin where it breaks down to carbon dioxide and water.

Some labels say the packaging is 'made from sustainable forests'. This indicates that new trees were planted to replace those cut down. However, this doesn't necessarily mean the product is 'environmentally friendly' unless it also states 'from managed forests' as the replacement trees may not be suitable for native wildlife. In addition, newly planted and immature trees do not offer the same conditions for wildlife as the mature trees they replace, and there's no guarantee the new trees will be allowed to reach maturity.

GENETICALLY MODIFIED (GM) INGREDIENTS

Many shoppers want to avoid foods they regard as environmentally unfriendly such as genetically modified products. GM foods come from unique strains of animals and plants created using laboratory techniques, rather than traditional farming methods such as cross-breeding. Environmental groups that oppose GM products claim:

* long-term health risks from eating GM food are still unknown and
* releasing GM organisms into the wild will have a detrimental environmental impact.

Any GM ingredients or derivatives must be listed. In the case of pre-packed foods, the label must say, 'This product contains genetically modified organisms,' or similar.

GM EXCEPTIONS

GM ingredients do not need to be stated on the label in the case of:

* products from animals fed on GM animal feed
* products made with GM technology (such as GM enzymes for cheese or baked foods)
* GM substances that are introduced accidentally or technically unavoidable, provided they do not add up to more than 0.9 per cent of the total (if accidental, food makers must prove they took reasonable steps to prevent it)
* additives that serve no technical function in the finished product
* additives used as processing aids, solvents or media for additives or flavouring.

If a food contains more than one GM ingredient, then 'genetically modified' must appear alongside each one ('produced from genetically modified soya', for example). The label must also state if a product was derived from a genetically modified plant or animal, such as 'contains rapeseed oil from genetically modified rape'. Non-pre-packed food and small containers must display GM information on a label placed nearby.

CHECKOUT...

When shopping for groceries, many consumers are understandably concerned about 'green' issues such as animal welfare, sustainability, environmental impact and fair trade with Third World producers. Many food makers are eager to promote their 'green' credentials, so always check:

* that animal welfare claims are certified by a recognised authority, and find out what level of welfare that represents
* that 'environmental' claims have the stamp of a recognised authority
* that packaging can be recycled and, if so, that you know where to take it
* that you can identify animal-derived ingredients if buying vegetarian or vegan products.

See also Chapters 2 and 6.

9

SHOPPING
FOR THE FAMILY

In many ways, buying family groceries couldn't be easier. There is a huge range of time-saving, labour-saving and flavoursome foods specifically designed to appeal to children of all ages. Snacks and convenience foods in particular are a boon for a typical modern family, where individual members like to eat different foods at various times of day.

Some parents never use fresh, unprocessed ingredients at all – except, perhaps, on special occasions such as Christmas or when entertaining. As a consequence, the total amount of time spent preparing a meal from scratch has declined over the years.

Convenience foods are more expensive than home-made meals. They may be highly processed, stripped of nutrients such as fibre, vitamins and minerals, and packed with saturated fat, added sugar and salt and chemical additives. That doesn't mean consumers should buy only unprocessed food but it does mean they should be selective. Convenience foods vary widely in content so by reading the label you can choose the healthiest brands.

SNACK FOODS

Snacks are designed to tickle the taste buds and satisfy the appetite and so tend to be high in sugar, salt and fat. Under pressure from Government and consumer groups, some food makers now limit levels of 'unhealthy' ingredients. For example, a major biscuit maker has cut salt by 20 per cent across its 15 best-selling products, and a leading crisp manufacturer has cut salt levels by 25 per cent.

This is welcome news. But unless you take time to compare products and choose the 'healthier' versions, you won't benefit from these changes. One concern is the salt content of children's snack foods. There are strict rules governing the salt content of formula milk and baby foods, but no such restrictions regarding snacks aimed at small children – even toddlers. High salt consumption impacts directly on child health, and once youngsters develop a taste for salty foods these dietary habits tend to continue into adulthood, with increased health risks in later life.

The pressure group Consensus Action on Salt and Health (CASH) looked at the salt content of children's snacks. Of the 10 popular brands studied, some contained over four times the level of salt that the FSA regards as 'high' – even for adults. According to CASH, children as young as three may consume up to

MAXIMUM DAILY SALT LEVELS FOR ADULTS AND CHILDREN

Women should have no more than 5g salt per day and men no more than 7g salt per day. For children, the recommended daily maximums are (by age):

Years	Max. salt/day
0–1	1g
1–3	2g
4–6	3g
7–10	5g
11+	5g

Figures based on FSA guidelines.

10g of salt per day – five times the recommended maximum for their age. A high-salt diet has an indirect effect by making a child thirstier and so increasing the amount of sugary drinks consumed, adding to the risks of obesity and tooth decay. Reducing a child's salt consumption therefore has short-term and long-term health benefits.

CRISPS AND SAVOURY SNACKS COMPARED

You can reduce your family's monthly consumption of salt, fat and sugar significantly just by switching brands. Bucks County Council Trading Standards studied leading brands of potato snacks, maize snacks and onion rings and found big differences:

Salt Levels

Products with the most salt were well above the FSA's 'high' rating (1.5g per 100g).

Highest	6.4g per 100g
Lowest	0.2g per 100g
Difference	*6.2g*

Fat Levels

Products with the most fat were well above the FSA's 'high' rating (20g per 100g).

Highest	38.7g per 100g
Lowest	1.4g per 100g
Difference	*37.3g*

Sugar Levels

Even savoury snacks had sugar levels approaching the Government's 'high' rating (15g per 100g).

Highest	12g per 100g
Lowest	0.2g per 100g
Difference	*11.8g*

CEREAL BARS COMPARED

Cereal bars are popular with both adults and children as 'breakfast on the go', and an energy 'fix' to get you through the mid-morning and mid-afternoon slumps. Some brands are aimed at adults, whereas others are targeted at children and added to countless school lunch boxes each day. One consumer group analysed 20 cereal bars for their sugar, total fat, saturated fat and salt content. Many exceeded official 'high' levels:

Sugar Levels

All had sugar levels well above the FSA's 'high' rating (15g per 100g).

Highest	41g
Lowest	17g
Difference	*24g*

Total Fat

Only one bar had total fat levels above the FSA's 'high' rating (20g per 100g). However, it was one of the lowest in terms of saturated fat.

Highest	22.8g
Lowest	6.8g
Difference	*16g*

Saturated Fat

More than half the bars tested had saturated fat levels above the FSA's 'high' rating (5g per 100g) and the highest had more than double this level.

Highest	11g
Lowest	2g
Difference	*9g*

Salt

Just as there is a surprising amount of sugar in savoury foods, so there can be a lot of salt in sweet products. None of the cereal bars tested had salt levels above the 'high' rating (1.5g per 100g) but there was a big difference between highest and lowest.

CHILDREN'S LUNCH BOXES

In surveys, only 25 per cent of school lunch boxes met standards set for school dinners. Over 90 per cent were too high in fat, had twice the maximum sugar level, up to half the maximum salt levels, and not enough fruit and vegetables.

For 7–10 year olds, the FSA recommends the following maximum levels per meal:

Fat	21.7g
Sugar	16.3g
Salt	1g

Limit salty or sugary snacks to a couple of packets per week and:

Replace...	with...
High-sugar snacks	Fresh fruit, such as apples, bananas, grapes, fresh fruit salad, small box of raisins
High-salt snacks	Fresh vegetables such as cherry tomatoes, sticks of carrot, cucumber, celery and peppers
Cola and juice drinks	Bottled water, unsweetened fruit juice, milk, yoghurt drink
Biscuits, cakes, chocolate	Currant buns, scones, fruit bread

Highest	1.15g
Lowest	Trace
Difference	*1.15g (approx.)*

As well as comparing brands and choosing the healthiest you should also aim to limit the processed snacks you buy and opt for healthy alternatives. For example, pretzels and rice crackers are both lower in fat than crisps but still provide an energy boost. And by replacing high-sugar/fat/salt snacks with fruit, or chopped raw vegetables (perhaps with a tasty low-fat dip), you also increase your intake of vitamins, minerals and fibre.

CONVENIENCE FOODS

Convenience foods require little time and effort to prepare. They include 'ready meals' and tinned soup that just need heating up, and foods such as fish fingers that need no preparation and minimal cooking. Many firms are making their convenience meals healthier. One food maker has reduced the salt in ready meals by 40 per cent. There are lots of healthy convenience foods too, such as ready-made salads and ready-prepared vegetables, so nutrition needn't be sacrificed for convenience.

READY MEALS

Supermarkets often include ready meals in their 'healthy eating' ranges. However, even 'healthy' ready meals may have high levels of salt, sugar and fat.

Where supermarkets follow the FSA's traffic light system (see page 53) it should be easy to compare brands and choose the healthiest. In the case of GDA-promoting brands (see page 54), comparisons are more difficult. To choose, it will be necessary to study the ingredients list and nutritional information box.

Tips for Healthy Ready Meals

Some ready meals may not satisfy all your nutritional needs on their own but there are ways to make them healthier:

* Portion sizes are often designed for the average woman, and contain too little energy for a teenage male or man. A male who doesn't need to lose weight could add an extra portion of starchy foods such as potatoes, pasta, rice or a slice of bread to fill himself up and so avoid the temptation of bingeing on high-Calorie foods.

* Adding a side portion of vegetables or salad makes a meal more filling, too, and boosts the vitamin and mineral content.

* Instead of eating a high-Calorie meal by your-self, you could share it with a companion and add extra vegetables and starchy foods to make up the energy gap.

* Have a starter of salad with low-fat dressing, or a platter of crunchy, raw, sliced carrot, broccoli, cauliflower florets, baby sweet corn, and red and green peppers, served with a spicy low-fat dip. This is enjoyable and adds vital nutrients.

SHOPPING FOR THE FAMILY

FATTY NUGGETS

Bucks County Council Trading Standards officers analysed bread-crumbed meat products, such as chicken nuggets, sold at supermarkets and take-away outlets. They found that the saltiest had nearly three times as much salt as the least salty, and fat levels differed by a factor of eight! Even more worryingly, many were high in trans fats (see page 20).

Salt

Highest	1.55g per 100g
Lowest	0.53g per 100g
Difference	*1.02g*

Fat

Highest	22.5g per 100g
Lowest	2.7g per 100g
Difference	*19.8g*

None of the labels indicated levels of salt and trans fats in the food. So, if the food makers won't tell you what you want to know about a product – don't buy it!

COATED PRODUCTS

Coated fish products may seem ideal for family meals. Fish fingers, for example, are easy to fry, grill or bake. They are mostly made from white fish, which is a low-Calorie source of protein, and have a tasty bread-crumb coating that appeals to children. But they vary widely in the levels of salt and fat they contain.

Bucks County Council Trading Standards officers analysed 300 brands of fish fingers and similar coated fish products. All were well above the Government's 'low' category for fat and, more alarmingly, only 12 of the brands tested were within the official 'low' category for saturated fat (less than 1.5g per 100g). Most were 'medium' (1.5–5g per 100g) and one was 'high' (over 5g per 100g – or over 5 per cent).

Salt levels varied, too. None was in the 'low' category (less than 0.3g per 100g). One brand was close to the 'high' salt category (more than 1.5g per 100g), which for children aged four to six years is half the recommended maximum daily salt intake of 3g. For younger children the figure is even lower. If served with beans, which can be up to 1.4g salt per 100g according to brand, a single meal can contain a child's maximum daily salt intake.

Total Fat

The difference between the highest and lowest levels of total fat in the fish fingers tested was:

Highest	17g per 100g
Lowest	5.3g per 100g
Difference	*11.7g*

Saturated Fat

The difference between the highest and lowest levels of saturated fat in the fish fingers tested was:

Highest	8g per 100g
Lowest	0g per 100g
Difference	*8g*

┌─────────────── **UNHEALTHY PRICE** ─┐
Price is no guide to 'healthy' products. The most
expensive bread-crumbed fish products often have
the most saturated fat, while the cheapest may
have the least.
└─────────────────────────────────────┘

Salt

There was a marked difference between the highest
and lowest salt levels in the fish fingers tested:

Highest	1.27g per 100g
Lowest	0.51g per 100g
Difference	*0.76g*

AVOIDING PROBLEM ADDITIVES

It is a fact of shopping life that the foods a family likes
best tend to be high in chemical additives. Of course
some additives are useful. They protect food from
toxins such as botulism (produced by a bacterium,
Clamydia botulinum) that once made tinned and
bottled foods risky. Additives also extend shelf life and
reduce spoilage, so cutting costs.

However, some people are sensitive to additives
and suffer allergies or 'allergy-like' symptoms including breathing difficulties, stomach upsets and nettle
rash (urticaria). Most at risk are those who also have
food allergies, asthma or a sensitivity to aspirin. The
worst offenders are sulphite, benzoate additives and
tartrazine.

Additives can have more than one scientific name, so to avoid confusion they are given an 'E number'. Those with an 'E' prefix can be used in all EU countries (but may be banned elsewhere). Many food makers avoid using the 'E' number, preferring to list the chemical name instead. Additives are listed by category (colouring, for example), so when studying food labels, first look for its category and then its name or 'E' number.

ACCEPTABLE DAILY INTAKE (ADI)

All additives are given an acceptable daily intake (ADI) rating that sets a limit on the amount that should be consumed in any one day. The ADI is based on its 'NOEL', or 'no observed (adverse) effect level' – the highest level before health problems occur – based on research on animals and humans. The NOEL is then scaled down to give a 'safe' ADI for a normal-weight adult. The ADI is lower for children, pregnant women and ill people, and may be reduced if new research suggests a substance poses more of a risk than first thought.

WHEN IS AN ADDITIVE NOT AN ADDITIVE?

Additives are substances added to foods to alter their flavour, colour, consistency and so on, but not regarded as traditional ingredients. Herbs and spices are not additives when used as flavourings, but are if used as colourings (such as curcumin). Additives in animal feed that end up in food products do not have to be declared.

Vitamins and minerals are not additives if used to make foods more nutritious or to replace natural ingredients lost in cooking, processing or storage, but are if added for another reason. For example, ascorbic acid (vitamin C) occurs naturally in fruit and vegetables and can be made synthetically or by genetic engineering. It is used as an antioxidant and anti-browning agent (to prevent oxidation/spoilage), preservative (to retain the natural colour of meat) and improving agent (in bakery products).

Flavourings do not have an 'E' number and need not be named unless a specific flavour has been listed on the label ('cheese and tomato flavour'). Flavourings are mainly used to enhance the taste of bland natural foods or replace flavour lost in cooking and/or processing. They may be natural extracts of foods, or synthetic but chemically identical to natural extracts, or wholly synthetic and unlike anything occurring in nature. The Hyperactive Children's Support Group advises its members that all flavourings should be avoided unless clearly labelled as natural extracts.

Most additives cause no ill effects. Some cause ill effects in a minority of people only. Mixtures of several additives may also cause problems. To limit the risk, try to choose foods with the fewest additives.

THE FEINGOLD DIET

Dr Ben Feingold was working in the allergy department of a San Francisco hospital when he found evidence linking diet with hyperactivity and other behavioural problems in children, such as attention deficit hyperactivity disorder (ADHD). His research focused on natural foods containing salicylates (aspirin-like compounds), and additives such as azo dyes. Sensitive children tended to:

* have difficulty sleeping and cry or scream excessively
* show poor feeding patterns and get very thirsty
* be impulsive and show lack of fear in risky situations
* exhibit aggressive or antisocial tendencies
* become restless, easily distracted, unable to concentrate and perform badly at school.

Dr Feingold treated the children by banning soft drinks and 'natural salicylates', such as almonds, apples, citrus fruit, cucumber, peaches, plums, prunes and tomatoes. He also eliminated artificial colouring, flavouring and other additives from the diet, especially benzoic acid, glutamates, BHA and BHT (see page 173). Many of Dr Feingold's recommendations are endorsed by the Hyperactive Children's Support Group.

PROBLEMATIC ADDITIVES

The following additives may cause one or more symptoms in sensitive people or be unsuitable for those with a medical condition. Those marked Ca are banned in some countries (but not the UK) following studies on animals that suggest possible carcinogenic (cancer-causing) risks.

Key to additives:

A   may trigger asthma attack and other symptoms

Al   may cause allergic reactions

Asp avoid if sensitive to aspirin

BC   unsuitable for babies and small children

Ca   possible carcinogen

CRS Chinese restaurant syndrome (see box, page 176)

D   may cause digestive upset

H   may cause hyperactive behaviour

KL   unsuitable for those with kidney and/or liver disease

M   may trigger migraine attacks

S   may cause skin swelling

U   may cause urticaria (nettle rash)

Colouring

Colouring enhances the appearance of some foods (such as yoghurt), or replaces colour lost in cooking or processing (such as tinned vegetables). Some colourings are natural, such as beetroot red, caramel (heated sugar), chlorophyll (green plants) and cochineal (crushed beetles). Others are chemically identical but synthetic ('nature identical'). The most controversial, azo dyes, are wholly artificial and were developed originally for the textile industry. They are used to create garish hues for children's foods. Colouring is found in squash, fizzy drinks, pie fillings, instant desserts and custard, convenience meals, cake mix, cough and cold remedies, jams and jellies, soups and sauces, salad dressing, sweets, ices, smoked fish, Scotch eggs and more.

COFFEE WITH CREAM, NOT COLOURING

Foods that must not contain added colouring include butter, coffee and tea, cream, milk (tinned, condensed, dried), fish and meat (raw/unprocessed), flour, fruit and vegetables (whole/unpeeled), fruit juice/nectar, game/poultry (raw/unprocessed), honey, suet and sugar. Colouring is not allowed in foods for babies and infants, except as vitamins (such as riboflavin) or 'pre-vitamins' (such as beta-carotene) that turn into vitamins in the body.

E102	tartrazine, FD&C yellow 5	A, Al, AS, H, U
E104	quinoline yellow	H, U
E110	sunset yellow FCF, orange yellow S	Al, AS, Ca, D, H, S, U
E120	cochineal, carminic acid, carmines, carmine of cochineal, natural red 4	H

E122	azorubine, carmoisine	A, Al, AS, H, S, U
E123	amaranth, red 2	A, AS, Ca, H, U
E124	ponceau 4R, cochineal red A, brilliant scarlet 4R	A, AS, H
E127	erythrosine, FD&C red 3	BC, Ca, H
E128	red 2G	H
E129	allura red AC	H
E131	patent blue V, acid blue V	Al, H, U
E132	indigo carmine, indigotine, FD&C blue 2	Al, D, H, U
E133	brilliant blue FCF	H
E142	green S (acid brilliant green)	H
E150 (a–c)	caramel colour, caustic sulphite caramel, ammonia caramel, plain/spirit caramel (not caramelised sugar)	H
E151	brilliant black BN, black PN, food black	H
E153	vegetable carbon, carbon black	Ca
E154	brown FK, food brown, kipper brown	Ca, H
E155	brown HT, chocolate brown HT	A, AS, H, U
E160 (b)	annato, bixin, norbixin	H, U
E161 (g)	canthanxanthin	H

| E173 | aluminium | H |
| E180 | pigment rubine, linthol rubine BK | H |

TARTRAZINE

Tartrazine is an azo dye that turns soft drinks and foods yellow, or is mixed with other dyes to create shades of cream, orange or green. It is used in cakes, custard, icing, jam, jelly, mustard, pickle, puddings, salad dressing, sauces, smoked fish, sweets and tinned vegetables. Tartrazine can cause a runny nose, nettle rash, eczema and asthma, and is associated with hyperactivity in children. It should be avoided by those with asthma and aspirin sensitivity. Its use is tailing off as food makers switch to other colourings.

Preservatives

Preservatives help extend the shelf life of foods by inhibiting mould (sulphur dioxide), bacteria (nitrates) or both (benzoic acid). People who are highly sensitive to certain preservatives may suffer symptoms such as digestive upset, breathing difficulties or skin rashes. Preservatives are used in beer, cured meat, fruit juice, jams, pickles, salad dressings, soft drinks, sweet sauces and wine, among other products.

| E210 | benzoic acid | A, AS, D, H, U |
| E211 | sodium benzoate, benzoate of soda | A, AS, H, U |

E212	potassium benzoate	A, AS, H, U
E213	calcium benzoate, monocalcium benzoate	A, AS, H, U
E214	ethyl para-hydroxybenzene, ethyl-4-hydroxybenzoate	A, H, U
E215	sodium ethyl para-hydroxybenzoate, ethyl-4-hydroxybenzoate, sodium salt	A, H, U
E216	n-propyl para-hydroxybenzoate, propyl 4-hydroxybenzoate	A, H
E217	sodium propyl para-hydroxybenzoate, propyl 4-hydroxybenzoate, sodium salt	A, AS, H, U
E218	methyl para-hydroxybenzoate, methyl-4-hydroxybenzoate, sodium salt	A, H
E219	sodium methyl para-hydroxybenzoate, methyl-4-hydroxybenzoate, sodium salt	A, H
E220	sulphur dioxide	A, Al, AS, D, H, KS
E221	sodium sulphite	A, Al, AS, D, H, KS

BENZOATES

Benzoates occur naturally in fruit and honey. They're also made synthetically and added to soft drinks and foods such as jams, pickles and syrups to protect against bacteria and fungi. They should be avoided by anyone with aspirin sensitivity, asthma and eczema, especially children, as they may worsen these conditions. The risk is greatest when found with sodium bisulphite (sodium hydrogen sulphite, or E222).

E222	sodium hydrogen sulphite, sodium bisulphite, acid sodium sulphite	A, Al, AS, D, H, KS
E223	sodium metabisulphite	A, Al, AS, D, H, KS
E224	potassium metabisulphite, potassium pyrosulphite	A, Al, AS, D, H, KS
E226	calcium sulphite	A, Al, AS, D, H, KS
E227	calcium hydrogen sulphite, calcium bisulphite	A, Al, AS, D, H, KS
E228	potassium hydrogen sulphite	A, Al, AS, D, H, KS
E230	diphenyl	H
E231	orthophenylphenol	H
E232	sodium orthophylphenate	H
E234	nisin	H
E235	natamycin	H

───────── **SULPHITES** ─────────

Sulphur dioxide and other sulphites must be labelled on food and drinks that contain more than 10mg per kilogram or litre, or if compound ingredients contain sulphites. This includes wines that contain more than 1.2 per cent alcohol (which is most of them), although they do not have to list other additives.

Sulphur-based chemicals are used as preservatives in soft drinks, dried fruits (dried apricots, raisins and sultanas) and meat products (burgers and sausages). They occur naturally in beer and wine making or are added to stop fermentation. They may trigger abdominal pain, diarrhoea, skin rash, a tight chest and breathing problems in asthmatics and aspirin-sensitive people. Sulphur dioxide gas in wine collects in the space under the cork and may trigger an asthma attack when the bottle is opened.

E249	potassium nitrite	BC, Ca, H
E250	sodium nitrite	BC, Ca, H
E251	sodium nitrate, Chile saltpetre	BC, Ca, H
E252	potassium nitrate	BC, Ca, D, H, KS
E261	potassium acetate, potassium ethanoate	KS
E280	propionic acid	M, U

NITRATES AND CANCER RISK

Nitrates are found in smoked, salted, cured and pickled foods. Potassium nitrate (saltpetre), for example, is used to preserve cured meats. The nitrate is converted to nitrite which, together with muscle pigment, gives bacon and salt beef their distinctive red colour. There may be a link between eating too many nitrate-containing foods and cancer. Nitrites are converted by bacteria in the gut into cancer-causing nitrosamines (which are found in tobacco smoke, too). When the Japanese consumed a lot of smoked/pickled foods they had a high incidence of stomach cancer. The Japanese now follow a more Westernised diet and the rate of this cancer is falling.

E281	sodium propionate, sodium propanoate	M, U
E282	calcium propionate, calcium propanoate	H, M, U
E296	malic acid, DL-malic acid, L-malic acid	BC

Antioxidants

Antioxidants such as vitamins C and E prevent fats and oils reacting with oxygen ('oxidation') and going rancid. They stop apple juice turning brown ('anti-browning agents'). Antioxidants are found in fruit-and-vegetable-based foods, cooking fat, vegetable oil and foods such as biscuits, cheese spread, chips, crisps, margarine, pastry, soft drinks and ready meals.

E310	propyl gallate, propyl ester of gallic acid, propyl 3,4,5-trihydroxybenzoate	A, Al, AS, BC, D, H, U
E311	octyl gallate	A, Al, AS, BC, D, H, U
E312	dodecyl gallate, dodecyl 3,4,5-trihydroxybenzoate	A, Al, AS, BC, D, H, U
E320	butylated hydroxyanisole, BHA	A, BC, H
E321	butylated hydroxytoluene, BHT	A, BC, H

Sweeteners

Sweeteners are used along with, or instead of, sugar to add sweetness to products. They are found in many processed foods including baked products, cake mix, chewing gum, cream cheese, fizzy drinks, fruit-flavour gums and jelly sweets, ice cream, jellies, milk drinks, salad dressing, sauces, soups, sweets and tinned vegetables.

Sweeteners have many other uses in food manufacturing and so are listed numerically along with the following:

Humectants, Stabilisers, Thickeners, Emulsifiers, Sequestrants

These often bizarre-sounding additives ensure food

┌─────────────── ARTIFICIAL SWEETENERS ───┐

'Intense' sweeteners are low-Calorie alternatives to sugar in sweet foods and drinks. Those used most commonly in the UK are: aspartame, saccharin, acesulfame potassium (acesulfame K), cyclamates and sucralose. Avoid consuming too many products containing bulk (or 'nutrative') sweeteners such as polyols (sorbitol, maltitol, mannitol, isomalt and xylitol), often found in 'diabetic foods' and sugar-free confectionery, as they have a laxative effect. For safety, try to vary the artificially sweetened products you buy so the family doesn't exceed its acceptable daily intake (ADI, see page 162).

└──┘

products keep the right consistency until you are ready to eat them. Humectants stop sweets and icing drying out and hardening, for example. Stabilisers stop yoghurts and jams separating and going runny. Pectin is a stabiliser that occurs naturally in fruit and is used in jam-making, when it is called a 'gelling agent'.

Stabilisers keep the head on fizzy drinks, including beer. Along with thickeners, they make 'watery' foods thicker, such as soups, sauces, pies and gravies. Natural thickeners include agar (seaweed), guar gum (from the guar plant) and starch.

Emulsifiers help fats and oils mix with water, such as in chocolate, ice cream, salad cream, margarine and packet soups. They can be made from natural gums and plant cellulose (such as lecithin and tragacanth), or synthetic soap-like substances (stearates). Sequestrants (or chelating agents) help remove metals such as iron and copper that enter food from metal containers and processing equipment. If left in place, metals can cause harmful chemical reactions, such as oxidation.

E413	tragacanth (gum tragacanth or gum dragon)	Al
E414	gum arabic (gum acacia or Sudan gum)	Al
E420 (i–ii)	sorbitol, sorbitol syrup	BC, D
E421	mannitol, manna sugar	BC, D
E950	acesulfame potassium, acesulfame K	BC, H
E951	aspartame	BC, Ca, H
E952	cyclamate, cyclamic acid and its Na and Ca salts	BC, H
E953	isomalt	BC, D, H
E954	saccharine and its Na, K and Ca salts	BC, H
E957	thaumatin	BC
E965 (i–ii)	maltitol, maltitol syrup	BC, D, H
E966	lactitol, sucralose	BC, D, H
E967	xylitol	BC, D
E968	erythritol (*currently awaiting EC approval*)	BC, D

Flavour Enhancers

Flavour enhancers boost the salty or 'meaty' flavour of foods and are often found in meat pies, sauces, sausages, snacks, soups and, most famously, Chinese food (see box).

E620	L-glutamic acid, alpha-aminoglutaric acid	Al, BC
E621	monosodium glutamate, sodium hydrogen L-glutamate (MSG)	Al, BC, CRS
E622	monopotassium glutamate, potassium hydrogen L-glutamate (MPG)	Al, BC, CRS, D, KL

CHINESE RESTAURANT SYNDROME

Monosodium glutamate is associated with an unpleasant food sensitivity reaction called Chinese restaurant syndrome (or Kwok's disease). Symptoms include a tight chest, dizziness, fainting, headache, nausea, numbness, palpitations and sweating.

| E623 | calcium glutamate, calcium dihydrogen di-L-glutamate | BC |
| E627 | disodium guanylate, guanosine 5' disodium phosphate | BC |

| E631 | disodium 5' inosinate, inosine 5' disodium phosphate | BC |
| E635 | disodium 5'-ribonucleotides | BC |

Glazing Agents

Glazing agents give a shiny finish to biscuits, sweets, cakes, pastries and edible cake decorations, and some are used as ice cream flavourings. They also have a preservative effect. They include beeswax (from honeycomb) and shellac (from insects).

TODDLERS AND TANTRUMS

A 2000 study by the Asthma and Allergy Research Centre (only recently released) looked at the effect of additives on a group of 277 three year olds. Over 14 days the children drank orange juice containing additives (at lower doses than in children's foods and drinks) followed by 14 days of additive-free juice. Parents didn't know which drink was which and just recorded behaviour in a diary. A quarter of the children exhibited more disruptive behaviour, including temper tantrums, during the two weeks they drank additive-laced juice. Additives used were preservative sodium benzoate (E211) and colourings tartrazine (E102), sunset yellow (E110), carmoisine (E122) and ponceau 4R (E124).

E901	beeswax, white and yellow	Al, U
E903	carnauba wax	Al, U
E904	shellac	Al, U

CHECKOUT...

Family shopping has never been so convenient – or so complicated. The most popular, easiest-to-prepare foods may be heavily laden with fat, sugar and additives. When buying food for the family, check:

* different brands of snacks and choose ones lowest in fat, sugar and additives
* that your children's school lunch box contains mostly healthy ingredients such as fruit, vegetables and wholemeal carbohydrates and fewer high-fat, high-sugar snacks
* that ready meals are not too high in sugar and fat, and add extra vegetables to boost the nutritional content
* the ingredients list for additives thought to cause health and/or behaviour problems in children, and avoid them.

See also Chapters 2 and 10.

10

SHOPPING FOR DIETARY NEEDS

Many people today need to take special care when buying foods because a member of the family has a food allergy or intolerance, or other ongoing medical condition. Some ingredients known to cause health problems must be displayed in the title ('tinned crab', for example) or listed in the ingredients. Labels must state if these ingredients are present, even if used as processing aids or present in an altered form. They are:

* celery, including celery spice and celeriac (celery root)
* cereals containing gluten (such as wheat, rye, barley, oats, spelt and kamut)
* eggs
* fish
* milk, from cow's, buffalo, goat or sheep milk and derivatives (such as milk solids, skimmed milk powder)
* mustard seeds, leaves and sprouted seeds

* nuts (almonds, brazils, cashews, hazelnuts, macadamias, pecans, pistachios, Queensland nuts and walnuts) and unrefined nut oils
* peanuts (listed separately from 'nuts', as peanut allergy is more common)
* shellfish – crustaceans and molluscs (such as prawn, crab, crayfish, lobster and mussels)
* sesame seeds
* soya and products such as soya milk, miso, tofu and tempeh
* sulphur dioxide/sulphites or SO2 (a preservative – see page 171) when present at more than 10mg per kilogram. This includes alcoholic drinks containing more than 1.2 per cent alcohol by volume (shown as '1.2% ABV').

If extracts are used, the origin may be given, such as 'whey (from milk)', 'casein (milk protein)', 'couscous (wheat)'. If there is more than one problem ingredient, each may be marked with an asterisk (*) and the origin given at the end (for example, '* from eggs').

WARNING BOX

Ingredients that pose a health risk may be listed in a separate box under the title of 'Warning!' or 'Allergens'. *A warning box is not compulsory* so never assume problem ingredients will be highlighted. Always check the label.

Allergens: Contains mustard, soya and egg.

Warning! May contain minor bones.

A warning box may indicate that a problem ingredient could have entered a product accidentally through 'cross-contamination', when the same manufacturing equipment is used to make different products. Some food makers attempt to limit their liability by putting blanket warnings on labels, such as, 'may contain traces of seeds or nuts!' or 'produced on a line handling milk, soya, gluten, mustard'. This makes life hard for people who react to these ingredients as it restricts the products they can buy.

PROBLEM-FREE PRODUCT LISTS

Many food makers and supermarkets have responded to public concern by producing foods on 'guaranteed safe' lines that are never used for problem ingredients. You can get special 'free from' lists from nearly all the major supermarket chains, including Asda, Co-op, Marks & Spencer, Morrisons, Sainsbury's, Somerfield, Tesco and Waitrose. These show own-brand foods that are, for example, free from egg, gluten, milk or nuts. Many food makers produce 'free from' lists, too, and some specialise in 'free from' ranges.

RULES FOR
NON-PRE-PACKED FOODS

Non-pre-packed food products do not need to list allergens. They include:

* bakery products sold loose (such as bread rolls)
* delicatessen foods sold from a shop or supermarket counter (such as sliced meats)
* sandwiches made to order (to be eaten straightaway)
* takeaway foods from a restaurant (if made on the premises)
* weighed foods sold loose (such as fruit and vegetables).

Foods that are sold loose pose a greater risk of cross-contamination from allergens such as nuts because the same knife or spoon may be used to prepare or serve different products, thereby transferring traces of allergen. Never buy loose foods when shopping for people who react badly to certain ingredients unless you know they are safe.

FOOD ALLERGIES

A food allergy occurs when the body's immune system becomes sensitised to a protein in food. This protein is then treated like a foreign invader, such as a parasite, and attacked. The chemical histamine is released, causing a local reaction, such as itching, tingling, a rash or blisters, especially of the mouth (oral allergy syndrome). Sometimes histamine triggers a flood of other chemicals that spread through the body causing a general reaction, known as anaphylaxis.

Food allergy symptoms vary but may include:

* tingling
* numbness or swelling of the lips, tongue, mouth or throat
* burning in the mouth
* skin flushing
* red itchy rash
* eczema
* red, itchy, swollen eyes
* runny nose
* nausea
* abdominal pain
* diarrhoea
* difficulty swallowing and speaking
* alterations in heart rate, including palpitations.

Anaphylaxis may cause severe asthma, a sense of impending doom, weakness and unconsciousness. Breathing or swallowing difficulties and/or collapse are a medical emergency needing immediate hospital treatment. Phone 999.

SHOPPING FOR ALLERGY SUFFERERS

When shopping for a dinner or children's party, always check in advance whether any guest has a food allergy. You could, for example, print a short form to include with the party invitations, which guests fill in and return with their RSVPs. You'll then have all the information to hand when you shop. Although fatal allergic reactions to food are rare, up to 2 per cent of adults and 6 per cent of pre-school children have food allergies. Each year, thousands of people suffer severe reactions, many needing hospital care. If a guest is allergic to any food, don't buy it – even if you plan to keep it separate from other food. 'Safe' food is easily 'contaminated' or a sufferer may eat it by mistake. In highly sensitive people, a reaction can be triggered just by touching or kissing someone who has eaten a food, such as peanuts, or entering a room where a food such as fish was prepared.

PRODUCT ALERTS

Check the ingredients of familiar products from time to time, and don't assume they are always going to be safe as food makers may change a recipe without warning. The Food Standards Agency website carries a regularly updated list of products whose ingredients have changed or contain unlisted allergens by mistake. Recent alerts include:

* fish products that now contain egg yolk powder
* Chinese egg fried rice containing unlisted prawns
* chocolates containing unlisted nuts
* tortilla chips containing unlisted milk
* vegetable spring rolls containing unlisted prawns
* organic burgamix containing unlisted mustard.

MULTIPLE FOOD ALLERGY

Having a multiple food allergy can make it difficult to find safe foods to eat. If you have to exclude a wide range of food groups from your diet, talk to a registered dietitian. They will draw up a diet plan that includes plenty of safe alternatives to ensure you get the quantity and range of nutrients you need for health.

CEREAL ALLERGY

Allergy to wheat is more common than allergy to other cereals, but barley, oats and rye may affect sensitive people too. As wheat allergy is sometimes confused with gluten intolerance (coeliac disease, see page 198), always see a doctor to get an accurate medical diagnosis if you react badly to a cereal product.

Cereal grains, flour and derivatives, such as gluten and starch, are found not only in baked foods but also in products such as burgers, sauces, sausages and soups. To avoid products containing cereals, check the label for barley, oats, rye, wheat and their flours, gluten and starch (such as 'wheat starch' or 'wheat flour'). Choosing 'gluten-free' foods may not protect wheat allergy sufferers, who can be allergic to other wheat proteins.

FISH AND SHELLFISH

Allergy to fish products is more common in adults than children. Any fish can cause an allergy, but especially anchovies, cod, salmon, sole and tuna, and products made from them. People who are allergic to cod are often allergic to haddock, hake, mackerel and whiting, too. Cooking does not remove fish allergens and may actually intensify them.

Shellfish that commonly trigger allergic reactions are clams, crabs, crayfish, lobsters, mussels, oysters, prawns, scallops and shrimps, as well as processed seafood products. Sensitive people may react to inhaled particles of raw or cooked fish in the air and suffer symptoms after entering a kitchen in which a piece of fish has been prepared.

OMEGA-3 ALLERGY

If you are allergic to fish, avoid products containing fish-derived omega-3 oils. Omega-3 is added to products such as yoghurt, yoghurt drinks and spreads. If a food contains omega-3 from fish then the word 'fish' must be listed in the ingredients.

EGG ALLERGY

Egg allergy is common, especially in children, but most outgrow it by school age. It causes a range of symptoms. In sensitive people, just inhaling microscopic particles of egg protein can trigger a severe reaction, so being in a kitchen where eggs have been prepared poses a risk. Principal egg allergens are conalbumin, ovalbumin and ovomucoid, all found in egg white (albumen). Egg yolk contains only minor allergens. Cooking or pasteurisation may destroy some allergens but not all. Raw, powdered and dried eggs are used as cheap protein to bind ingredients, and as pastry-browning agents. Cholesterol-free egg replacements may contain egg white. Egg derivatives include albumen, globulin, ovovitelin, silico albuminate and vitelin.

ALFRED DEFEATS THE YELLOW PERIL

Alfred Bird, a chemist living in Birmingham in the 19th century, found a clever answer to his wife's dilemma. She adored egg custard but was allergic to eggs. In 1837, Alfred made custard using corn-flour instead of egg to act as a binding and thickening agent. Bird's Custard became very popular – even with non-allergy sufferers.

PEANUT ALLERGY

Allergy to peanuts can cause a rapid and severe reaction and is a common cause of anaphylactic shock. Just handling an object touched by someone who has traces of peanut on their hand can trigger symptoms. The peanut is a legume so peanut allergy sufferers may be allergic to other members of the legume family, such as:

* beans, including baked beans, bean sprouts, string beans, soya beans and soya products (such as tofu)
* peas and lentils, including chickpeas and houmous
* liquorice sweets (liquorice is a legume)
* carob and carob syrup (used in chocolate sweets)
* fenugreek (a herb used in curries and Middle Eastern dishes)
* additives such as E413 (tragacanth) and E414 (gum acacia).

Peanut allergy sufferers may also react to lupin seeds and flour, used in bread, pasta and pastry products (see 'Lupin Allergy', page 194). Peanuts may be added to foods as a cheap form of protein. They are common in Eastern-style ready meals and may be used instead of pine nuts in pesto sauce. Peanut-derived ingredients are added to cosmetics and medications, often under different names. For example, peanut oil is also known as groundnut oil and – in cosmetics – as arachis oil. Peanut oil is less risky than peanut protein, but highly sensitive people may still be at risk (see box, opposite). Some oil mixtures contain peanut oil, so avoid foods that say 'blended oil' on the label.

UNREFINED PEANUT OIL

Refined or 'gourmet' peanut oil contains little peanut protein and so may be safe for peanut allergy sufferers. However, unrefined peanut oil may still pose a risk, so avoid all peanut oil unless you know for sure it is safe.

NUT AND SEED ALLERGY

Nuts are often called 'tree nuts' on labels to distinguish them from peanuts. Brazil nuts, almonds and hazelnuts are common causes of nut allergy, but cashews, macadamias, pecans, pine nuts, pistachios and walnuts may also trigger a reaction. A nut allergy is usually for life. Unless you know you react to only one type of nut it is best to avoid them all. Nuts are used in biscuits, cakes and puddings, and added to breakfast cereals, meat-free foods (such as vegetarian burgers and sausages), pesto sauce and Waldorf salad. Nut allergy sufferers may also be allergic to poppy and sesame seeds and coconut.

NUT AND SEED OILS

Highly refined vegetable oils have had all the allergenic proteins removed and so are safe for allergy sufferers. Common ingredients used in oils found in pre-packed foods are maize, palm, rapeseed, sunflower and soya. Speciality seed and nut oils – such as peanut, sesame and walnut, often made using a cold-press method – are not so highly refined and so may cause symptoms in sensitive people.

MILK ALLERGY

Allergy to cow's milk is the most common food allergy in childhood, affecting up to 7 per cent of babies aged under 12 months, and is regularly misdiagnosed by doctors. Babies, children and adults may suffer a reaction to milk itself, one of the proteins it contains or milk sugar (lactose). Therefore, it is important to seek medical advice to discover the underlying cause. Most children grow out of milk allergy by school age but it can continue into adulthood. Milk allergy can cause abdominal pain, nausea, vomiting and diarrhoea, runny nose and/or sneezing, bronchitis, asthma and wheezing. Eczema is also common. Rarely, milk allergy causes anaphylaxis.

Look for these milk-derived products: milk solids,

FORMULA MILK

If your baby has cow's milk allergy, always seek the advice of your GP or health visitor about a suitable alternative you can use. Many formula milks and baby foods contain cow's milk protein and so may be unsuitable. Partially hydrolysed milk and soya formulas can also trigger symptoms in some babies. Milk from other species, such as sheep and goat, lacks iron and other nutrients a baby needs. Milk products containing skimmed milk and non-milk fat that have not been formulated for infants must display the warning that they are unsuitable for babies and small children.

skimmed milk powder, curds (the dense component in milk), whey (the watery component left behind when curds are removed), whey solids, casein, caseinate, potassium caseinate, lactalbumen and lactoglobulin. The proteins in goat, sheep and buffalo milk are similar to cow's milk and may also cause symptoms. Ask your doctor or dietitian to suggest alternatives that provide similar levels of vitamins and minerals.

CELERY ALLERGY

Allergy to celery stalks and celery root (celeriac) can cause symptoms from mild oral allergy to anaphylactic shock (although this is rare). Celery, celeriac and the spices and seasonings made from them (celery salt and celery spice), are common ingredients in a wide range of foods. Sensitive people may react to all celery products.

MUSTARD AND SPICE ALLERGY

Mustard allergy is rare in the UK and symptoms are usually mild. Foods may contain mustard seed powder, mustard oil, sprouted mustard seeds (as in mustard and cress) and ingredients derived from leaves and flowers. Long-lasting products, such as pickles, sauces and condiments containing unlisted mustard, can still be found on food shelves. Some people are allergic to other spices, including caraway, coriander, fennel, paprika, saffron, garlic and chives. Hay fever sufferers who react to birch pollen and mugwort are at higher risk of spice allergy.

SESAME SEED ALLERGY

Sesame seeds and products derived from them are sprinkled onto biscuits, bread, buns, cakes and other bakery products for flavour and decoration. Sesame seeds are also used in popular dips and accompaniments in Eastern and Middle Eastern dishes, such as houmous and tahini. People allergic to sesame seeds may react to other seeds (especially poppy seeds), nuts (hazelnuts) and cereals (rye). Sesame oil is unrefined and so will also cause symptoms in allergy sufferers. It is often brushed on to speciality breads ('tiger paws') and other baked foods as a browning and flavouring agent, as well as being an ingredient in many processed foods and ready meals.

SOYA BEAN ALLERGY

Soya beans are being added to an ever-growing range of foods. Inevitably, as more children get exposed to soya at a younger age, so more are becoming allergic. Most children grow out of it by school age but many sufferers keep the allergy into adulthood. Food makers often use textured soya protein as a meat substitute – particularly in vegetarian meals – and as a meat extender to increase the protein and improve texture.

Soya protein and flour are used as alternatives to cereals, dairy foods, eggs, sauces and wheat. Soya flour is also added to baked foods as a preservative and browning agent. Refined soya oil is found in some blended vegetable oils, but the refining process makes it safe for allergy sufferers. Soya milk formulas were once used as an alternative to cow's milk. As soya milk allergy has become more common, formula milk makers have switched to hydrolysed casein. Never give soya milk to a baby without first checking with your doctor or health visitor. Soya allergy sufferers may also react to beans, lentils, peas, peanuts, and barley and rye flour.

OTHER FOOD ALLERGENS

The following are some of the less common causes of food allergy.

Corn (Sweet Corn or Maize) Allergy

Corn is sold as corn on the cob, and as frozen and tinned sweet corn, and is used in pizza toppings, breakfast cereals, biscuits, cake mix, ice cream cones and some types of batter. It is the basis of cornflour, used to thicken soups, sauces and puddings.

LATEX-FOOD SYNDROME

People who are allergic to latex (natural rubber) may react to certain fruits and nuts (called latex-food syndrome). The reason for this is unknown but there are two theories. There may be allergens in latex that mimic those found in fruits, nuts and spices. Or it may be that fruit pickers and packers who wear latex gloves accidentally transfer small particles of latex to the produce, triggering allergic symptoms when the food is eventually eaten.

Fruit and Vegetable Allergy

Fruit and vegetables that cause allergies include apples, avocados, bananas, berries (especially straw- berries), carrots, celery, citrus fruits, kiwi fruit and very ripe tomatoes. Fruit and vegetable allergies are becoming more common, especially among hay fever sufferers. Allergy to the pollen of birch trees and some non-flowering wild plants may also lead to allergy to fruit (such as apples and kiwi fruit). Symptoms are usually mild. Cooked fruit and pasteurised fruit juices are usually safe as heating destroys the allergens.

UBIQUITOUS KIWI

Kiwi allergy was little known in the UK 30 years ago but is now on the rise, especially in children, as the fruit becomes more widely used in yoghurt, juices, purées, fresh and tinned fruit salad, cakes and other desserts.

Lupin Allergy

Lupin seeds are traditional ingredients in continental foods sold in speciality shops. The seeds are sprinkled onto bread as a flavouring and decoration, and lupin flour is added to other flours to boost the protein in cereal-based foods, including batter and pasta (espe- cially spaghetti). As lupin flour becomes more widespread, allergic reactions to it are growing more common. Symptoms vary from mild to severe, including (rarely) anaphylaxis. Peanut allergy sufferers may react to lupin seeds, and vice versa.

Meat Allergy

Meat allergy sufferers can react to one type of meat or several. Cooking may not destroy the allergens. Some products such as sausages, frankfurters, luncheon meat, pâtés and pies contain more than one type of meat, making it hard to identify specific allergens. If you are allergic to processed meat but not individual pieces of meat, there may be other ingredients responsible for your symptoms, such as cereals (used in burgers and sausages) and milk (used in bread crumb coatings).

Mycoprotein Allergy

Mycoprotein (such as Quorn™), from an edible fungus, is used in meat-free products, such as vegetarian bacon, sausages and burgers. The most common allergy reaction is abdominal pain. Less commonly there may be vomiting, nettle rash and breathing difficulties. The full extent of the problem is unknown as mycoprotein products are easily identifiable and people who try it a few times and react badly (such as the author of this book) may simply stop using it and not report their symptoms. People who are allergic to mushrooms and other fungi, including hay fever sufferers who react to airborne fungal spores, may be allergic to mycoprotein.

Pine Nut Allergy

Pine nuts (kernels) are seeds rather than nuts, so seed allergy sufferers may need to avoid them. People who are sensitive to peanuts, almonds and other nuts may be allergic to pine nuts, and vice versa.

Rice Allergy

Allergy to rice is uncommon in the West but more common in the East where rice is the staple crop. As more people in the UK eat rice regularly, so rice allergy may increase.

BEWARE 'NATURAL' HISTAMINE

Histamine is not only released as part of an allergic reaction. It can also occur naturally through the action of bacteria on poorly stored raw seafood. This can trigger allergy symptoms but it is not an allergy as such – and so may affect anyone.

PROTECTING YOURSELF

If you suffer a severe reaction to food you must take steps to protect yourself:

* Make sure anyone who may buy food for you knows what you are allergic to.
* Tell dinner companions about your allergy and ask them in advance to avoid any food that might put you in danger.
* Wear a MedicAlert necklet or bracelet at all times.

This provides details of your medical condition and a 24-hour emergency contact number.

FOOD INTOLERANCE

Many people today need to take special care when buying foods because a family member has a food allergy or intolerance, or other diet-related condition, such as diabetes. A food allergy is a severe immune system reaction to a food ingredient. Once individuals become 'sensitised' to a food they will always react to it – even tiny amounts. A food intolerance is caused by a non-allergic reaction to food, for example, owing to a lack of the enzyme needed to digest it. In this case how badly individuals react to a food depends on several factors, such as the amount they consume.

FRUCTOSE INTOLERANCE

Some people have difficulty digesting fructose, a sugar found in fruit and some vegetables and also added to processed foods as 'high fructose corn syrup' (see page 21). 'Dietary fructose intolerance' or 'fructose malabsorption' causes symptoms such as abdominal pain, bloating, flatulence and diarrhoea or constipation. This condition is not the same as 'hereditary fructose intolerance' which can cause severe illness.

Naturally occurring fructose in vegetables such as green beans, leek and onions usually poses few problems. Even natural foods that are very high in fructose, such as honey, fruit juice and dried fruit, may be tolerated in small amounts. A more serious problem is posed by high fructose corn syrup, which contains up to 38 per cent fructose and is added to soft drinks and many processed products including biscuits, cakes, dessert puddings, sweets, yoghurts and cough medicine. Check the ingredients list for high fructose corn syrup, corn syrup or glucose-fructose syrup.

GLUTEN INTOLERANCE

Gluten is a mixture of two proteins, gliadins and glutonins, formed when flour is mixed with water. Some people have an intolerance or 'hypersensitivity' to gluten and must avoid it. Symptoms may be mild and infrequent or severe. This is coeliac disease, an 'auto-immune disease' in which the body's immune defences attack the gut lining, causing inflammation and damage and inhibiting absorption of nutrients. The condition can strike at any age, from infancy to adulthood, but is most often diagnosed between the ages of 40 and 50.

Symptoms include abdominal discomfort and pain, bloating, diarrhoea, excess wind and vomiting. There may be weight loss and deficiencies of some vitamins and minerals, leading to iron-deficiency anaemia and tiredness. In children, it can affect growth and development. If untreated, the condition may lead to infertility, osteoporosis and cancer. Some people suffer gluten-related eczema (dermatitis herpetiformis).

> ─── GLUTEN-FREE LOGO ─
> A dark blue 'ear of wheat' logo means that a food is
> free of gluten from wheat, rye or oats. All the major
> supermarkets stock gluten-free foods.

People who are highly sensitive to gluten must avoid all foods containing wheat, rye and barley, as well as less-common types such as spelt and kamut. This includes wheat bran, flour, rusk and starch; barley malt and flour; and rye flour. Oats contain a similar protein but it is not the same. Some people can tolerate oats whereas others must avoid it as well as products (such as oat bran) derived from it. However, oat crops and food products are sometimes cross-contaminated by wheat during harvesting or processing.

Substitute foods, such as gluten-free bread, flour and pasta, are available. Other forms of carbohydrate may be okay, such as buckwheat, corn, millet, potatoes and rice. Take care with processed foods, though. Gluten is found in burgers, batter, bread-crumb coating, sausages, soups and sauces. All pre-packed foods that contain gluten must list it in the ingredients.

Manufacturers may use the term 'wheat', 'rye', 'barley' or 'gluten'; or 'wheat gluten'. If a product contains modified starch containing gluten it must say 'wheat starch' on the label. Even naturally 'gluten-free' foods may contain up to 20 parts per million gluten as a small degree of contamination can occur.

Maltodextrins are made from corn/maize starch, wheat starch, tapioca or rice. They contain little gluten and so are not toxic for a gluten-free diet. Despite the name, they are not produced from and don't contain barley malt. Malt extract and malt extract flavourings, made from barley, are widely used as flavour enhancers in the food industry. The amount of malt extract or malt flavouring used varies. People with coeliac disease should avoid products containing a high percentage of malt extract, such as malted drinks. Small amounts, in malted rice breakfast cereals and malt vinegar, are tolerated by most sufferers. All products that contain barley must say so. Get expert advice if unsure.

Glucose syrup and other forms of sugar made from wheat can be safely eaten, so food makers do not need to list 'glucose syrup (from wheat)' in the ingredients list. Processing (hydrolysation) removes almost all gluten from the final product.

GLUTEN-FREE PRODUCTS

The following ingredients are gluten-free: artificial sweeteners, caramel, corn malt, dextrose, glucose syrup, isomalt, maize starch, maltitol, maltodextrin, rice malt and rice rusk. If you are very sensitive to gluten, see your doctor or dietitian before following a restrictive gluten-free diet.

> ── AVOID WHEAT-FREE! ──
>
> 'Wheat-free' *does not* mean 'gluten-free'! A 'wheat-free' product may still have other gluten-containing cereals including barley or rye. Avoid if sensitive to gluten.

LACTOSE INTOLERANCE

Lactose is a disaccharide (that is, it comprises two sugars – glucose and galactose). It occurs naturally in milk. Some people lose (or never acquire) the ability to digest lactose. Undigested, it is a laxative and passes unchanged into the bowel, where it is acted on by gut bacteria to produce hydrogen gas. This causes symptoms such as abdominal pain, swelling (bloating), nausea, sickness, flatulence and diarrhoea. This condition, lactose intolerance, should not be confused with cow's milk allergy.

As people get older, their ability to digest lactose often declines and, from middle age onwards, they may switch to alternatives, such as soya or rice milk. Adults may develop temporary lactose intolerance after food poisoning, or as a side-effect of coeliac disease, Crohn's disease or inflammatory bowel disease (IBD).

> ## ── 'NATURAL' LACTOSE INTOLERANCE ──
>
> Although most people in northern Europe can digest milk, lactose intolerance is common else-where, especially Eastern and Southern Europe, Africa and Asia. As the UK now has such a broad racial mix, it is a good idea to check with dinner guests beforehand whether they can tolerate milk.

Symptoms of lactose intolerance vary, depending on severity. Many people tolerate dairy products such as yoghurt and hard cheese. These contain little or no lactose as the sugar is broken down during processing. Some people can cope with small quantities of milk, such as in milk chocolate or the milk glaze on pastries.

Adults can live without lactose. 'Lactose-free' and 'reduced-lactose' products are available in supermarkets and health-food shops. There is no legal limit to the amount of lactose in 'reduced-lactose' products, but official guidelines say there should be at least 25 per cent less than in dairy milk. Alternatives to dairy milk include soya milk and rice- and oat-based drinks, which are lactose-free. Choose brands fortified with calcium, vitamins and minerals as they are as nutritious as milk.

Lactose is added to various foods including biscuits, cakes, puddings and ready meals. Look on labels for lactic acid (E270), lactic acid esters (E472b), calcium lactate (E327), milk solids, skimmed milk powder, sodium lactate (E325), whey or whey solids.

DIABETES

Diabetes is very common and yet shrouded in myths, especially over food. In fact, a person with diabetes simply follows the kind of healthy diet suitable for everyone. Diabetes is a condition in which blood glucose levels rise too high. Blood glucose is controlled by hormones, especially insulin. Type 1 diabetes occurs when the cells that make insulin are destroyed. If these cells make some insulin, but not enough, or the muscles, liver and fat tissue refuses to react to the insulin that is made, type 2 diabetes occurs. A third type, gestational diabetes, can develop in pregnancy.

People with diabetes may feel constantly thirsty, need to urinate more than usual (especially at night), get very tired, lose weight, have blurred vision and suffer genital itching and/or thrush. In many cases, though, there are no symptoms and the condition only comes to light during a routine blood test. Type 1 is managed with diet, insulin and exercise. Type 2 is managed through diet and exercise and often tablets and insulin too.

SHOPPING FOR DIABETICS

When studying food labels, try to keep the following in mind: people with diabetes need regular, balanced meals (including healthy snacks) based around fruit, vegetables and starchy carbohydrates to keep blood sugar levels as even as possible. Keep fat, salt and sugar to a minimum. Ideally, meals should be healthy *and* enjoyable so no one feels they are 'missing out'. When shopping, visualise three food shelves, as follows:

* Bottom shelf filled with vegetables and fruit – at least five different types. These make up a third of the meal (or half the meal for those trying to lose weight).
* Middle shelf filled with bread, rice, pasta, potatoes and other starchy carbohydrates. These make up a third of all meals.
* Top shelf divided between dairy foods (milk and cheese), protein foods (meat, fish, beans, peas, lentils and so on), and a small amount of fatty/sugary foods. These make up the remaining third of all meals (or less for those trying to lose weight).

Here are some additional points to bear in mind when shopping for diabetics:

Vegetables and Fruit

Vegetable and fruit products are healthy, filling, low in Calories and delicious, so buy plenty. Fresh, frozen and tinned fruit and vegetables all count. Tinned vegetables can be high in salt so drain and rinse then add fresh water before heating. Choose tinned fruit in juice, not syrup, and spread the fruit intake throughout the day to avoid raising blood glucose too quickly. Fruit juice contains important vitamins and minerals so it is more beneficial than drinks containing sugar and flavourings alone (and counts towards the recommended 'five-a-day'). However, it can still raise blood sugar rapidly and so should be drunk once daily only, ideally with a meal.

'Starchy' Carbohydrates

Starchy carbohydrates ('carbs') release glucose at a steady rate and help avoid the rapid highs and lows caused by sugary foods. Choose mainly high-fibre whole grain types that prevent constipation and lower blood cholesterol. Starchy carbs are naturally low in fat but some have added fat, such as ciabatta, chapattis, nan bread and croissants (check the label if pre-packed). They make a tasty occasional treat but avoid buying them too often, especially for those who have to watch their weight.

Vary the carbohydrates to make meals interesting. Choose from rice, pasta, sweet potatoes, bulgar wheat, couscous and noodles. Other kinds include buckwheat, a good source of fibre, protein, vitamins and minerals; wild rice, which is high in protein, vitamins and minerals and often mixed with other types of rice; and quinoa, which is cooked like rice and has all eight essential amino acids plus essential fatty acids.

Opt for baked foods that are low in fat and sugar, such as crumpets, muffins, fruit bread, morning coffee biscuits, ginger nuts, malt loaf, rich tea biscuits, scones and tea cakes. Cereal bars are handy for a quick energy boost, especially to prevent dangerously low blood sugar (hypoglycaemia or a 'hypo'), but check the label and avoid high-sugar, high-fat brands (see page 154).

GI FOODS

Some carbohydrates contain 'resistant starches' that take longer to convert into glucose after we eat them. This is useful, as they supply energy at a slower, steadier, sustainable rate. The glycaemic index (GI) is a way of rating foods such as carbohydrates according to how quickly they release glucose into the blood.

* Low-GI foods break down slowly and so are preferable to high-GI foods. They include basmati rice, easy cook rice, Granary™ bread, noodles, pasta, plantains, porridge, rye bread, sweet potato, wholemeal pitta bread and yams.
* High-GI foods include white and wholemeal bread, boiled and baked potatoes, cornflakes, crisped or puffed wheat and sugar-coated cereals.

There are websites that list the GI of all foods – including well-known brands (see page 218). This is especially important in the case of single foods, such as breakfast cereals. Bear in mind, though, that a balanced meal is a mixture of foods, and usually has a lower GI anyway.

Dairy Foods

Milk, cheese and yoghurt are rich in vitamins and minerals, especially calcium, but choose low-fat types where possible. Soya and rice milk are lower-fat alternatives to full-fat dairy milk but choose brands that have been fortified with calcium.

Meat, Fish and Other Proteins

Aim to vary protein foods in the diet. Choose lower-fat types, such as lean beef, turkey and chicken (without the skin), and replace some meat with non-meat alternatives, such as eggs, fish, nuts, pulses (peas, beans and lentils), Quorn™, seeds and tofu. Include oily fish regularly for a healthy heart. Make high-fat meat products, such as pies, fatty curries, creamy pasta sauces and toppings, rare treats only.

Fatty Foods

Check the label and limit or avoid products containing fatty meats, hard margarine and products high in palm oil. Look for foods generally lower in fats and oils and choose healthier types, such as olive oil, rapeseed oil, peanut oil, nut and seed oils. Low-fat gravy granules, vegetable-based sauces (such as tomato sauce) and oil-free dressings (containing, for example, lemon, vinegar and herbs) are better choices than high-fat meat-based gravy and oil-based dressings. Buy foods to grill, poach, steam, microwave, dry-roast or oven bake (all methods that don't need extra oil).

Sugary Carbohydrates

Sugar is a simple form of carbohydrate that causes a rapid rise in blood sugar. Sugary foods need not be excluded from the diet but aim to limit them. Choose reduced-sugar varieties of jams, or spread small amounts only on bread. Look for 'sugar-free', 'low-sugar', 'diet', 'reduced-Calorie' or 'reduced-sugar' products. Low-sugar foods may contain extra fat (and sometimes salt) to enhance the flavour, so always study the label.

Salt

Check food labels and avoid products high in salt. Don't add salt at the table and limit how much you add to cooking. Herbs and spices are better choices for flavouring meals and do not contain salt/sodium.

CHECKOUT...

Food allergies and intolerances are on the increase so it is important to know how to recognise problem ingredients on food labels. When buying food for family members or friends with dietary needs check:

* with a doctor if any food seems to cause serious symptoms, and never assume you know the cause
* the ingredients list – as well as the warning box – for problem ingredients
* the Food Standards Agency website for foods wrongly labelled as problem-free (see page 218)
* the websites of grocery chains and food manufacturers for ranges of 'free from' foods (see page 215)
* with a dietitian if you are having to exclude major foods groups from the diet.

See also Chapter 2 and Useful Websites (page 215).

FINAL NOTE

Only a few decades ago it was perfectly acceptable for food makers to give little or no indication of the ingredients on their products and make ambitious health-enhancing claims with little or no justification. Now food makers must list every ingredient and processing method, yet the claims they can make are becoming increasingly restricted. Some food makers would no doubt say this is 'bureaucracy gone mad!' but the pressure to make these changes has come mainly from shoppers, not bureaucrats.

Food labels are likely to get even more complex in the coming years, so we must all get into the habit of reading the label and learning what it all means. I hope this book has provided a useful insight into the intricacies and idiosyncrasies of food labelling. If you would like to know more, the following reading list and websites can provide useful additional information. *Bon appétit!*

FURTHER READING

Dietary Reference Values for food energy and nutrients for the United Kingdom. Report of the Panel on Dietary Reference Values of the Committee on Medical Aspects of Food Policy. UK Department of Health (1991).

Fats of Life, by Caroline M. Pond. Cambridge University Press, Cambridge (2003).

Human Nutrition: A Health Perspective, by Mary Barasi. Hodder Arnold, London (2003).

Labelling and Composition of Meat Products: Guidance Notes. Food Standards Agency (2003).

McCance and Widdowson's the Composition of Foods: Summary Edition, by Sir John Krebs. Food Standards Agency (2002).

Report of the IGDS/PIC Industry Nutrition Strategy Group Technical Working Group on Guideline Daily Amounts (GDAs). Institute of Grocery Distribution (2005).

Seven Countries: Death and Coronary Heart Disease, by Ancel Keys. Commonwealth Fund Publications (1980).

USEFUL WEBSITES

Allergy UK

www.allergyuk.org
This is the leading charity for people with allergy,
intolerance and chemical sensitivities. The website has
a help line, fact sheets, the latest food alerts and product recalls – plus contact details for food makers with
'free from' food lists.

Anaphylaxis Campaign

www.anaphylaxis.org.uk
This support group website for people with life-
threatening allergies contains useful information
including 'food alerts' detailing incorrectly labelled
food products.

ASDA

www.asda-health.co.uk/freefrom/freefrom.html
The supermarket's website provides lists of ASDA
products that do not contain problem ingredients,
including egg, glutamate, gluten, milk, nuts, shellfish,
soya and wheat.

Assured Food Standards

www.redtractor.org.uk

This website gives more information on the AFS assurance standards set for food and farming companies that are entitled to use the 'red tractor' logo on their products.

British Dietetic Association

www.bda.uk.com

This website provides the latest food news plus a wide range of fact sheets on all aspects of food and diet.

British Nutrition Foundation

www.nutrition.org.uk

This website has useful information on issues relating to many aspects of food science and health.

Coeliac UK

www.coeliac.co.uk

This charity helps people with coeliac disease and dermatitis herpetiformis through direct support, campaigns and research. The website provides advice and information on the condition and gluten-free products and services.

Compassion in World Farming

www.ciwf.org.uk

This farm animal welfare organisation campaigns to stop farm animal cruelty and end factory farming. Read background and contact information on this website.

Co-op Food

www.co-op.co.uk/foodretail/index.php?pageid_
grp=141
This address provides contact details to receive lists of
foods free from milk, soya, egg, nuts or wheat, or email
them directly at: customer.relations@co-op.co.uk

CORE – The Digestive Disorders Foundation

www.corecharity.org.uk
This website provides a range of fact sheets on various
digestive disorders including lactose intolerance and
coeliac disease.

Diabetes UK

www.diabetes.org.uk
Diabetes UK is the leading national charity for people
with diabetes. The Diabetes UK website has lots of
useful diet advice for people with diabetes.
www.storetour.co.uk
This address is their online 'store tour' guide to shopping and menu planning.

Dietitians Unlimited

www.dietitiansunlimited.co.uk
This website provides contact details of local independent freelance dietitians whom you can consult on
all aspects of personal diet and nutrition.

Ethical Junction Network

www.ethical-junction.org

The Ethical Junction website provides contact details of Fairtrade, organic and other ethical and sustainable food products and services.

Fairtrade Foundation

www.fairtrade.org.uk

This organisation licenses the 'Fairtrade' mark to companies that meet the ethical standards it sets regarding payments to Third World producers and sustainable farming. The website provides more information on Fairtrade products and suppliers.

Food Standards Agency

www.food.gov.uk

This site is packed with information on all aspects of food and nutrition, including frequently asked questions, and links to other useful websites.

Freedom Foods

www.rspca.org.uk

Use this website to find out more about the RSPCA's 'Freedom Food' charity, set up to improve animal welfare standards in the food and farming industries.

Glycaemic Index (GI)

www.glycemicindex.com

This website is the official 'home of the glycaemic index'. It carries a regularly updated database of carbohydrate foods with their glycaemic index rating. Low GI is up to 55, medium GI is 56 to 69 and high GI is from 70 to 100.

Hyperactive Children's Support Group

www.hacsg.org.uk

This website explains all about this group, which helps children and their families cope with hyperactivity and attention deficit hyperactivity disorder (ADHD).

LEAF – Linking Environment and Farming

www.leafmarque.com

This website provides useful background on integrated farm management and the 'LEAF' marque.

Marine Conservation Society

www.fishonline.org

The Marine Conservation Society's website provides up-to-date information on which fish are in short supply as well as a list of MSC environmentally certified fish products and the stores that sell them.

Medic Alert Foundation UK

www.medicalert.co.uk

The Medic Alert Foundation provides lifesaving identification bracelets and necklets for people with a serious hidden medical condition. The scheme is supported by a 24-hour emergency telephone service. The 'jewellery' opens to reveal medical and vital details, such as condition, blood group and medication, that first aid and medical personnel would need in an emergency.

Morrisons

www.morrisons.co.uk/1775.asp
This site tells you about Morrisons' range of 'free
from' own-label products.

Organic Farmers & Growers

www.organicfarmers.org.uk
This website gives background information on inspec-
tion and licensing of organic farming and food
processing in the UK.

Sainsbury's

www.sainsburys.co.uk/food/specialdiets/allergiesand
intolerance
This address takes you to the section on the
Sainsbury's website where you can find information
on special diets and download 'free from' own-label
and branded products. These include products free
from eggs, gluten, milk and wheat. Lists of nut-free
products are also available, by post or email: just
follow the instructions.

Soil Association

www.soilassociation.org
The Soil Association is the leading campaign group
promoting organic farming and foods and sets high
standards for organic produce that bear its logo. This
website gives background information on organic
foods and a link to the Organic Directory, which lists
outlets for organic produce throughout the UK.

Sustain: the Alliance for Better Food and Farming

www.sustainweb.org

This website gives background information on 'Sustain', a campaigning alliance of 100 organisations working to promote food and agriculture policies that enhance the health and welfare of animals, people and society in general.

Tesco

www.tesco.com/health/eating/?page=freeform

This website tells you about Tesco's range of 'free from' own-label products.

Vegan Society

www.vegansociety.com

This website has advice and information on shopping for animal-free food products, and details of special events such as 'Vegan Day'.

Vegetarian Society

www.vegsoc.org

The Vegetarian Society website has a wide range of information on vegetarianism, including download-able information sheets on avoiding non-vegetarian products and ingredients.

Waitrose

www.waitrose.com/food_drink/nutrition/specialdiets

This address takes you to the section on the Waitrose website where you can find information on special diets and download 'free from' own-label and branded products. These include products free from nuts, gluten, milk and lactose, plus there are helpful links to sites giving information on special diets and food allergies. You can receive personal information about diet and nutrition by emailing nutrition@waitrose.co.uk

INDEX